Collins

PRACTICE MULTIPLE CHOICE QUESTIONS

CSEC®
Human and
Social Biology

**Shaun
deSouza**

William Collins' dream of knowledge for all began with the publication of his first book in 1819.

A self-educated mill worker, he not only enriched millions of lives, but also founded a flourishing publishing house. Today, staying true to this spirit, Collins books are packed with inspiration, innovation and practical expertise. They place you at the centre of a world of possibility and give you exactly what you need to explore it.

Collins. Freedom to teach.

Published by Collins
An imprint of HarperCollins*Publishers*
The News Building
1 London Bridge Street
London
SE1 9GF

Browse the complete Collins Caribbean catalogue at
www.collins.co.uk/caribbeanschools

ISBN 978-0-00-827115-2

Practice Multiple Choice Questions: CSEC® Human and Social Biology is an independent publication and has not been authorised, sponsored or otherwise approved by **CXC®**.

CSEC® is a registered trademark of the **Caribbean Examinations Council (CXC®)**.

British Library Cataloguing in Publication Data
A catalogue record for this publication is available from the British Library.

Author: Shaun deSouza
Series editor: Anne Tindale
Publisher: Dr Elaine Higgleton
Commissioning editor: Tom Hardy
In-house senior editor: Julianna Dunn
Project manager: Alissa McWhinnie, QBS Learning
Copyeditor: Aidan Gill
Proofreader: Helen Bleck
Answer checking: Sara Hulse
Typesetter: QBS Learning
Illustrator: Ann Paganuzzi
Cover designer: Gordon MacGilp
Series designer: Kevin Robbins
Production controller: Tina Paul
Printed and bound by: Grafica Veneta SpA in Italy

MIX
Paper from
responsible sources
FSC™ C007454

This book is produced from independently certified FSC™ paper to ensure responsible forest management.

For more information visit: www.harpercollins.co.uk/green

The publishers gratefully acknowledge the permission granted to reproduce the copyright material in this book. Every effort has been made to trace copyright holders and to obtain their permission for the use of copyright material. The publishers will gladly receive any information enabling them to rectify any error or omission at the first opportunity.

Contents

Introduction

Structure of the CSEC® Human and Social Biology Paper 1 examination

There are **60 questions**, known as **items**, in the Paper 1 examination and the duration of the examination is **1 ¼ hours**. The paper is worth **40%** of your final examination mark.

The table below shows the approximate number of questions from each section of the syllabus.

Section	*Approximate* number of questions
A: Living organisms and the environment	5
B: Life processes	35
C: Heredity and variation	4
D: Disease and its impact on humans	8
E: The impact of health practices on the environment	8
Total	**60**

The Paper 1 questions test one profile, **knowledge and comprehension**. Questions will be presented in a variety of ways, including the use of diagrams, tables, data, graphs, prose or other stimulus material.

Each question is allocated 1 mark. You will not lose a mark if a question is answered incorrectly.

Examination tips
General strategies for answering multiple choice questions

- Read every word of each question very carefully and make sure you understand exactly what it is asking. Even if you think that the question appears simple or straightforward, there may be important information you could easily omit, especially small, but very important words such as *all* or *only*.
- When faced with a question that seems unfamiliar, re-read it very carefully. Underline or circle the key pieces of information provided. Re-read it again if necessary to make sure you are very clear as to what it is asking and that you are not misinterpreting it.
- Each question has four options, **(A)**, **(B)**, **(C)** and **(D)** and only one is the correct answer. Look at all the options very carefully as the differences between them may be very subtle; never stop when you come across an option you think is the one required. Cross out options that you know are incorrect for certain. There may be two options that appear very similar; identify the difference between the two so that you can select the correct answer.
- You have approximately 1 ¼ minutes per question. Some questions can be answered in less than 1 minute while other questions may require longer because of the reasoning or calculation involved. Do not spend too long on any one question.
- If a question appears difficult place a mark, such as an asterisk, on your answer sheet alongside the question number and return to it when you have finished answering all the other questions. Remember to remove the asterisk with a clean eraser once you have completed the question.
- Answer every question. Marks are not deducted for incorrect answers. Therefore, it is in your best interest to make an educated guess in instances where you do not know the answer. Never leave a question unanswered.
- Always ensure that you are shading the correct question number on your answer sheet. It is very easy to make a mistake, especially if you plan on returning to skipped questions.
- Some questions may ask which of the options is NOT correct or is INCORRECT. Pay close attention to this because it is easy to fail to see these key words and answer the question incorrectly.

- Some questions may give two or more answers that could be correct and you are asked to determine which is the BEST or MOST LIKELY. You must consider each answer very carefully before making your choice because the differences between them may be very subtle.
- When a question gives three or four answers numbered **I, II** and **III** or **I, II, III** and **IV**, one or more of these answers may be correct. You will then be given four combinations as options, for example:

  A   I only

  B   I and II

  C   I and III or II and III

  D   I, II and III

  Place a tick by all the answers that you think are correct before you decide on the final correct combination.

- Do not make any assumptions about your choice of options: just because two answers in succession have been **C**, it does not mean that the next one cannot be **C** as well.
- Try to leave time at the end of the examination to check over your answers, but never change an answer until you have thought about it again very carefully.

Strategies for the CSEC® Human and Social Biology Paper 1

- Calculators are not allowed in the examination. When answering a question that requires you to perform a calculation, work out the answer by writing your working on the question paper before you look at the options. If you do not find your answer in the options, you can then go back and re-check your working for mistakes.
- Some questions refer to a labelled diagram. Read and inspect the diagram carefully to make sure you know exactly which structure the label line is indicating before answering.
- Questions are taken from all areas of the syllabus for the multiple choice examination. Make sure you cover the entire syllabus in order to be able to answer all the questions that are asked.

Section A: Living organisms and the environment
A1: Living organisms and cells

1 Which of the following activities is defined as 'the breakdown of food to release energy'?

(A) nutrition   (A)

(B) respiration   (B)

(C) excretion   (C)

(D) photosynthesis   (D)

2 Which of the following is NOT a feature of ALL living organisms?

(A) Releasing metabolic waste products.   (A)

(B) Responding to environmental changes.   (B)

(C) Feeding to obtain or make energy-containing compounds.   (C)

(D) Moving from one place to another to obtain food.   (D)

3 A typical animal cell differs from a typical plant cell as the animal cell lacks

    I a cellulose cell wall.

    II a cell membrane.

    III chloroplasts.

    IV a nucleus.

(A) I only   (A)

(B) I and III only   (B)

(C) II and IV only   (C)

(D) I, II and III only   (D)

Items 4–5 refer to the diagram below, showing an unspecialised plant cell.

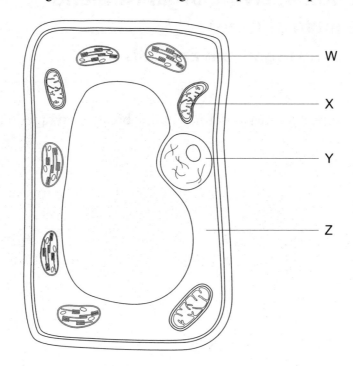

4 Identify the cellular structure labelled **X**.

(A) mitochondrion   (A)

(B) chloroplast   (B)

(C) cytoplasm   (C)

(D) nucleus   (D)

5 Which of the labelled structures is the site of photosynthesis?

(A) W   (A)

(B) X   (B)

(C) Y   (C)

(D) Z   (D)

6 Which organelle below is INCORRECTLY matched to its function?

	Organelle	Function	
(A)	ribosome	site of protein synthesis	Ⓐ
(B)	mitochondrion	site of respiration	Ⓑ
(C)	cell membrane	controls substances entering and leaving the cell	Ⓒ
(D)	endoplasmic reticulum	supports the cell when turgid	Ⓓ

7 Hyphae are thin filaments that form the body of a

(A) virus. Ⓐ

(B) fungus. Ⓑ

(C) bacterium. Ⓒ

(D) protozoan. Ⓓ

8 Which of the following statements about viruses is TRUE?

(A) They show all the characteristics of living organisms. Ⓐ

(B) They have an outer coat made of cellulose. Ⓑ

(C) They have membrane-bound organelles in their cytoplasm. Ⓒ

(D) They can only reproduce inside other living cells. Ⓓ

Item 9 refers to the following diagram, showing a specialised cell of the human body.

9 Which cell is shown in the diagram?

(A) muscle Ⓐ

(B) nerve Ⓑ

(C) sperm Ⓒ

(D) epithelial Ⓓ

10 Which of the following options shows the levels of organisation of the body in the correct sequence?

(A) cells ⟶ tissues ⟶ organs ⟶ organ systems   Ⓐ

(B) tissues ⟶ organ systems ⟶ cells ⟶ organs   Ⓑ

(C) cells ⟶ organs ⟶ organ systems ⟶ tissues   Ⓒ

(D) organ systems ⟶ organs ⟶ cells ⟶ tissues   Ⓓ

11 Which of the following processes is defined as 'the net movement of particles from a region of high concentration to a region of low concentration along a concentration gradient'?

(A) active transport   Ⓐ

(B) evaporation   Ⓑ

(C) osmosis   Ⓒ

(D) diffusion   Ⓓ

Item 12 refers to the following diagram, which shows an experiment to investigate osmosis.

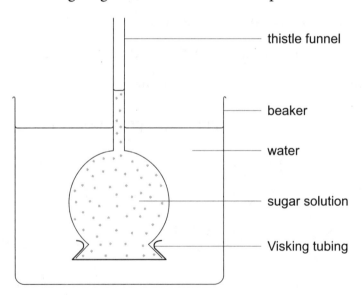

12 Which statement BEST describes what will be observed after 2 hours?

(A) The water level in the beaker will go up.   Ⓐ

(B) The water level in the beaker will remain the same.   Ⓑ

(C) The level of the sugar solution in the funnel will go up.   Ⓒ

(D) The level of the sugar solution in the funnel will go down.   Ⓓ

13 By which process does carbon dioxide enter the stomata of leaves?

(A) osmosis   Ⓐ

(B) diffusion   Ⓑ

(C) transpiration   Ⓒ

(D) active transport   Ⓓ

14 Which option in the table below tells us what will happen to plant cells and animal cells placed into water for a few hours?

	Plant cells	Animal cells	
(A)	burst	become turgid	Ⓐ
(B)	become turgid	shrink	Ⓑ
(C)	become turgid	burst	Ⓒ
(D)	shrink	shrink	Ⓓ

15 By which process do mineral ions enter root hair cells of plants?

(A) osmosis   Ⓐ

(B) diffusion   Ⓑ

(C) transpiration   Ⓒ

(D) active transport   Ⓓ

A2: Photosynthesis, food chains and cycles

1 What is the source of carbon for photosynthetic plants?

(A) glucose   Ⓐ

(B) methane   Ⓑ

(C) carbon dioxide   Ⓒ

(D) carbon monoxide   Ⓓ

2 All of the following factors are necessary for photosynthesis, EXCEPT

(A) water. Ⓐ

(B) oxygen. Ⓑ

(C) sunlight. Ⓒ

(D) carbon dioxide. Ⓓ

3 The main pigment in green plants that is responsible for absorbing sunlight is

(A) chlorophyll. Ⓐ

(B) chloroplast. Ⓑ

(C) mesophyll. Ⓒ

(D) palisade. Ⓓ

4 Glucose produced during photosynthesis is

    I used in respiration.

    II passed out by diffusion.

    III converted to starch for storage.

    IV converted to sucrose and transported around the plant.

(A) I and II only Ⓐ

(B) III and IV only Ⓑ

(C) I, II and III only Ⓒ

(D) I, III and IV only Ⓓ

5 Humans depend on plants for which of the following?

    I fuel

    II food

    III oxygen

    IV carbon dioxide

(A) II only Ⓐ

(B) II and III only Ⓑ

(C) I, II and III only Ⓒ

(D) I, II and IV only Ⓓ

6 Which of the following is a suitable definition for the term <u>trophic level</u>?

(A) A diagram showing feeding relationships in an ecosystem. Ⓐ

(B) The position at which an organism feeds in a food chain. Ⓑ

(C) The part of the ecosystem an organism occupies. Ⓒ

(D) Organisms and their interactions with the non-living environment. Ⓓ

<u>Items 7–8</u> refer to the food chain shown below.

hibiscus flower ⟶ butterfly ⟶ lizard ⟶ cat

7 Which organism shown is the secondary consumer?

(A) hibiscus Ⓐ

(B) butterfly Ⓑ

(C) lizard Ⓒ

(D) cat Ⓓ

8 Which of the following statements about the food chain is/are TRUE?

I The hibiscus is the producer.

II The butterfly occupies trophic level 2.

III An increase in the cat population will cause the lizard population to decrease.

IV An increase in the lizard population will cause the butterfly population to increase.

(A) I and II only Ⓐ

(B) III and IV only Ⓑ

(C) I, II and III only Ⓒ

(D) I, II and IV only Ⓓ

9 What is the initial source of energy for a food chain?

(A) the Sun Ⓐ

(B) the producer Ⓑ

(C) the consumer Ⓒ

(D) carbon dioxide Ⓓ

Items 10–11 refer to the food chain shown below.

phytoplankton $\longrightarrow$ coral $\longrightarrow$ butterfly fish $\longrightarrow$ snapper

10 Which organism in the food chain shown above will receive the LEAST energy?

(A) phytoplankton   Ⓐ

(B) coral   Ⓑ

(C) butterfly fish   Ⓒ

(D) snapper   Ⓓ

11 Which organism in the food chain is MOST likely to be a herbivore?

(A) phytoplankton   Ⓐ

(B) coral   Ⓑ

(C) butterfly fish   Ⓒ

(D) snapper   Ⓓ

12 The diet of wild monkeys consists of roots, insects, fruits and herbs. Wild monkeys can be described as being

(A) carnivores.   Ⓐ

(B) herbivores.   Ⓑ

(C) omnivores.   Ⓒ

(D) detritivores.   Ⓓ

13 Which of the following statements about energy flow through an ecosystem is/are INCORRECT?

    I Energy is recycled in ecosystems.

    II Organisms release energy during respiration.

    III Energy flows in one direction through ecosystems.

    IV Organisms lose energy to the environment as heat.

(A) I only   Ⓐ

(B) III only   Ⓑ

(C) I and II only   Ⓒ

(D) III and IV only   Ⓓ

Item 14 refers to the following diagram, which shows part of the carbon cycle.

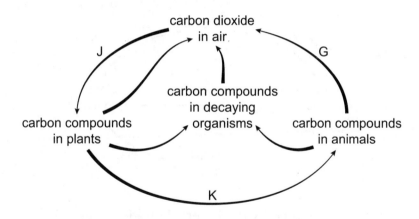

14 Which processes are represented by the letters G, J and K?

	G	J	K	
(A)	photosynthesis	respiration	ingestion	Ⓐ
(B)	ingestion	photosynthesis	respiration	Ⓑ
(C)	respiration	photosynthesis	ingestion	Ⓒ
(D)	respiration	ingestion	photosynthesis	Ⓓ

15 Which human activity below is correctly matched with its impact on the carbon cycle?

	Human activity	Impact	
(A)	burning of fossil fuels	reduced CO_2 in atmosphere	Ⓐ
(B)	deforestation	increased CO_2 in atmosphere	Ⓑ
(C)	population growth	reduced CO_2 in atmosphere	Ⓒ
(D)	overharvesting of animals	increased CO_2 in atmosphere	Ⓓ

Items 16–17 refer to the diagram below, which shows a simplified nitrogen cycle.

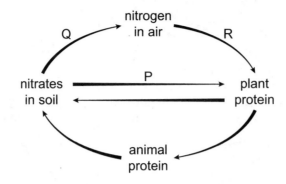

16 Which processes are represented by the letters P and R?

	P	**R**
(A)	nitrification	nitrogen fixation
(B)	assimilation	denitrification
(C)	denitrification	nitrification
(D)	assimilation	nitrogen fixation

Ⓐ
Ⓑ
Ⓒ
Ⓓ

17 Which organisms carry out the process labelled Q?

(A) nitrifying bacteria   Ⓐ

(B) denitrifying bacteria   Ⓑ

(C) ammonifying bacteria   Ⓒ

(D) nitrogen-fixing bacteria   Ⓓ

Section B: Life processes
B1: Nutrition (1)

1 Which of the following nutrients is made up of peptide chains?

(A) lipids   Ⓐ

(B) proteins   Ⓑ

(C) vitamins   Ⓒ

(D) carbohydrates   Ⓓ

2 Select the option below that lists the richest sources of carbohydrates.

(A) bread, cake, pasta   (A)

(B) fish fillet, ground beef, eggs   (B)

(C) orange, watermelon, mango   (C)

(D) butter, coconut oil, fried chicken   (D)

3 Which option in the table below correctly matches each nutrient to its final breakdown product(s)?

	Proteins	Lipids	Starch	
(A)	amino acids	glycerol	maltose	(A)
(B)	dipeptides	fatty acids and glycerol	glucose	(B)
(C)	polypeptides	fats	sucrose	(C)
(D)	amino acids	fatty acids and glycerol	glucose	(D)

4 Lipids are needed in the diet for all of the following, EXCEPT

(A) storage.   (A)

(B) insulation.   (B)

(C) as an energy source.   (C)

(D) growth and repair of tissues.   (D)

5 Which option below lists the main sources of vitamin C?

(A) lemons, cherries, pineapples, oranges   (A)

(B) liver, spinach, carrots, pumpkins   (B)

(C) oily fish, eggs, lean meat, butter   (C)

(D) peas, beans, nuts, brown rice   (D)

6 Bobby has weak bones, brittle nails and tooth decay. When he gets a cut, his blood takes a long time to clot. Which mineral may be missing from his diet?

(A) iron Ⓐ

(B) iodine Ⓑ

(C) calcium Ⓒ

(D) potassium Ⓓ

7 Ayana's diet is lacking in vitamin A. Which of the following deficiency diseases is she MOST likely to suffer from?

(A) rickets Ⓐ

(B) anaemia Ⓑ

(C) beri-beri Ⓒ

(D) night blindness Ⓓ

8 Which of the following vitamins is important in the prevention of rickets?

(A) vitamin A Ⓐ

(B) vitamin B_1 Ⓑ

(C) vitamin C Ⓒ

(D) vitamin D Ⓓ

9 Which of the following minerals will be recommended for someone who has been diagnosed with anaemia?

(A) iron Ⓐ

(B) iodine Ⓑ

(C) calcium Ⓒ

(D) potassium Ⓓ

10 Which of the vitamins listed below are classified as fat soluble?

      I vitamin A

     II vitamin B

    III vitamin D

    IV vitamin K

(A) I and II only   Ⓐ

(B) II and III only   Ⓑ

(C) I, III and IV only   Ⓒ

(D) II, III and IV only   Ⓓ

11 The table below shows the results of three tests carried out on a liquid food substance.

Test	Result
Benedict's reagent added; boiled using a water bath	colour change from blue to brick-red
iodine solution added	colour remains yellow/brown
sodium hydroxide solution added; dilute copper sulfate solution added	colour change from blue to purple

Which nutrients does the food substance contain?

(A) starch and lipid   Ⓐ

(B) protein and lipid   Ⓑ

(C) protein and reducing sugar   Ⓒ

(D) starch and reducing sugar   Ⓓ

12 A food item left a translucent mark when a drop of it was rubbed on absorbent paper and the paper was left to dry. Which nutrient does the food contain?

(A) lipid   Ⓐ

(B) starch   Ⓑ

(C) protein   Ⓒ

(D) non-reducing sugar   Ⓓ

13 Which of the following is NOT a role of water in the body?

    (A) to cause constipation   Ⓐ

    (B) as a transport medium   Ⓑ

    (C) to assist in the hydrolysis of food during digestion   Ⓒ

    (D) to dissolve waste substances so they can be excreted   Ⓓ

14 Which of the following are roles of dietary fibre in the body?

    I to stimulate peristalsis

    II to reduce the risk of colon cancer

    III to reduce the bulk of food in the digestive system

    (A) I and II only   Ⓐ

    (B) I and III only   Ⓑ

    (C) II and III only   Ⓒ

    (D) I, II and III   Ⓓ

15 Which food items listed below would be MOST likely to help prevent constipation?

    I apple

    II cabbage

    III white flour

    IV wholegrain cereal

    (A) I and II only   Ⓐ

    (B) III and IV only   Ⓑ

    (C) I, II and IV only   Ⓒ

    (D) I, II, III and IV   Ⓓ

16 A balanced diet consists of

(A) mostly fruits and vegetables.　Ⓐ

(B) food from most food groups.　Ⓑ

(C) food from all food groups in the same proportions.　Ⓒ

(D) food from all food groups in the correct proportions.　Ⓓ

17 Malnutrition results from

    I eating too much food.

    II not eating enough food.

    III improper hygiene in food preparation.

    IV eating nutrients in the wrong proportions.

(A) I and II only　Ⓐ

(B) II and III only　Ⓑ

(C) I, II and IV only　Ⓒ

(D) I, III and IV only　Ⓓ

18 A deficiency of protein in children causes

(A) bulimia.　Ⓐ

(B) anorexia.　Ⓑ

(C) marasmus.　Ⓒ

(D) kwashiorkor.　Ⓓ

19 Deena eats large amounts of food quickly. She then induces vomiting in order to lose weight. She is MOST likely to be suffering from

(A) bulimia.　Ⓐ

(B) anorexia.　Ⓑ

(C) marasmus.　Ⓒ

(D) kwashiorkor.　Ⓓ

20 The energy requirements of an individual depend on all of the following, EXCEPT

(A) age. Ⓐ

(B) height. Ⓑ

(C) gender. Ⓒ

(D) level of physical activity. Ⓓ

21 Which person from the options below would be expected to have the highest daily energy requirement?

(A) newborn baby Ⓐ

(B) professional athlete Ⓑ

(C) 5-year-old child Ⓒ

(D) office worker Ⓓ

22 The correct formula used in the calculation of Body Mass Index (BMI) is

(A) height/weight. Ⓐ

(B) $weight/height^2$. Ⓑ

(C) $weight^2/height$. Ⓒ

(D) $height^2/weight$. Ⓓ

B2: Nutrition (2)

1 Which type of tooth is matched correctly to its function in the table below?

	Type of tooth	Function	
(A)	canine	tears food	Ⓐ
(B)	incisor	crushes and grinds food	Ⓑ
(C)	molar	grips food	Ⓒ
(D)	premolar	cuts food	Ⓓ

Items 2–3 refer to the diagram below, which shows the teeth in the human upper jaw.

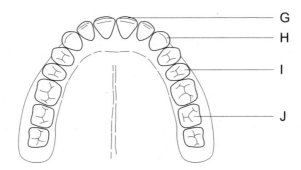

2 Which tooth is an incisor?

(A) G Ⓐ

(B) H Ⓑ

(C) I Ⓒ

(D) J Ⓓ

3 What is the function of the tooth labelled I?

(A) to grip food Ⓐ

(B) to cut and bite food Ⓑ

(C) to crush and grind food Ⓒ

(D) to tear off pieces of food Ⓓ

4 Which type of digestion is carried out by teeth?

(A) external Ⓐ

(B) chemical Ⓑ

(C) intracellular Ⓒ

(D) mechanical Ⓓ

Items 5–6 refer to the following section through a tooth.

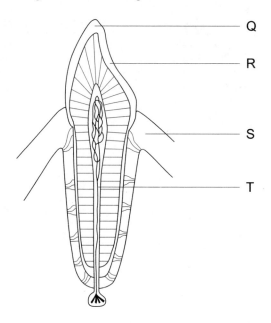

5 Q is the

(A) pulp cavity.

(B) dentine.

(C) enamel.

(D) gum.

    Ⓐ

    Ⓑ

    Ⓒ

    Ⓓ

6 Which labelled structure is similar to bone and forms the bulk of the tooth?

(A) Q

(B) R

(C) S

(D) T

    Ⓐ

    Ⓑ

    Ⓒ

    Ⓓ

7 All of the following activities contribute to tooth decay, EXCEPT

      I grinding the teeth.

     II using dental floss daily.

   III consuming sugary foods.

   IV consuming acidic fruit juices.

(A) I only   (A)

(B) II only   (B)

(C) I and II only   (C)

(D) III and IV only   (D)

8 All of the following are stages in the process of tooth decay, EXCEPT

(A) plaque is formed on the tooth.   (A)

(B) viruses in plaque produce acids.   (B)

(C) acids dissolve the outer layers of the tooth.   (C)

(D) a cavity is formed.   (D)

9 Which of the following minerals can be added to drinking water to reduce tooth decay?

(A) iron   (A)

(B) calcium   (B)

(C) chloride   (C)

(D) fluoride   (D)

10 Which of the following is NOT a property of enzymes? They

(A) are specific.   (A)

(B) can be inhibited by certain substances.   (B)

(C) remain unchanged at the end of the reaction.   (C)

(D) are unaffected by temperature changes.   (D)

11 Which of the following would be the MOST likely consequence if living cells did NOT produce enzymes?

(A) No chemical reactions would take place. Ⓐ

(B) Fewer chemical reactions would take place. Ⓑ

(C) Chemical reactions would take place at a slower rate. Ⓒ

(D) Chemical reactions would take place at a faster rate. Ⓓ

Items 12–13 refer to the graph below, which shows the effect of pH on the activity of four enzymes.

12 Which enzyme is MOST likely to be salivary amylase?

(A) I Ⓐ

(B) II Ⓑ

(C) III Ⓒ

(D) IV Ⓓ

13 In which part of the alimentary canal would the enzyme labelled I be MOST active?

(A) mouth Ⓐ

(B) stomach Ⓑ

(C) ileum Ⓒ

(D) duodenum Ⓓ

14 The enzyme amylase catalyses the conversion of

(A) starch ⟶ maltose   Ⓐ

(B) starch ⟶ glucose   Ⓑ

(C) maltose ⟶ glucose   Ⓒ

(D) protein ⟶ peptides   Ⓓ

15 Which of the following enzymes catalyses the breakdown of fat?

(A) pepsin   Ⓐ

(B) trypsin   Ⓑ

(C) lactase   Ⓒ

(D) lipase   Ⓓ

16 Arrange the words below in the sequence in which these processes occur in the human body.

    I – absorption   **II** – digestion   **III** – ingestion   **IV** – assimilation

(A) I ⟶ II ⟶ III ⟶ IV   Ⓐ

(B) III ⟶ II ⟶ I ⟶ IV   Ⓑ

(C) III ⟶ II ⟶ IV ⟶ I   Ⓒ

(D) II ⟶ III ⟶ I ⟶ IV   Ⓓ

17 The process by which food moves through the oesophagus is called

(A) mastication.   Ⓐ

(B) swallowing.   Ⓑ

(C) egestion.   Ⓒ

(D) peristalsis.   Ⓓ

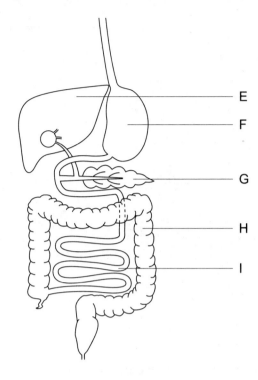

18 In which labelled structure does the digestion of protein begin?

(A) E   Ⓐ

(B) F   Ⓑ

(C) G   Ⓒ

(D) I   Ⓓ

19 Which labelled structure removes large quantities of water from undigested food?

(A) E   Ⓐ

(B) G   Ⓑ

(C) H   Ⓒ

(D) I   Ⓓ

20 Which structure contains villi?

(A) E   Ⓐ

(B) F   Ⓑ

(C) H   Ⓒ

(D) I   Ⓓ

21 Which of the following BEST describes the role of the liver in digestion?

(A) secretion of intestinal juice   Ⓐ

(B) transport of bile   Ⓑ

(C) production of bile   Ⓒ

(D) storage of bile   Ⓓ

22 The role of bile salts in the alimentary canal is to

(A) moisten and lubricate food.   Ⓐ

(B) emulsify lipids.   Ⓑ

(C) kill bacteria.   Ⓒ

(D) clot milk protein.   Ⓓ

23 Which waste material is produced when excess amino acids are broken down in the liver?

(A) urea   Ⓐ

(B) glycogen   Ⓑ

(C) glucose   Ⓒ

(D) nitrogen   Ⓓ

24 Glucose, produced by the body during digestion, can be

    I used in respiration.

    II used to make hormones.

    III converted to glycogen for storage.

    IV used to make cell membranes.

(A) I only   Ⓐ

(B) I and III only   Ⓑ

(C) II and III only   Ⓒ

(D) I, II and IV only   Ⓓ

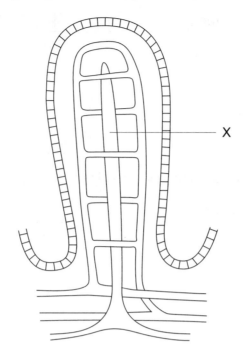

25 Which substance(s) is/are absorbed into X?

   (A) water   Ⓐ

   (B) amino acids   Ⓑ

   (C) monosaccharides   Ⓒ

   (D) fatty acids and glycerol   Ⓓ

26 Which of the following statements is TRUE?

   (A) Egestion is the removal of undigested food from the body.   Ⓐ

   (B) Excretion is the removal of undigested food from the body.   Ⓑ

   (C) Excretion and egestion refer to the same process.   Ⓒ

   (D) Egestion is a stage in the process of excretion.   Ⓓ

1 Breathing is important to humans in order to

    (A) remove carbon dioxide produced during respiration.   Ⓐ

    (B) supply carbon dioxide needed for respiration.   Ⓑ

    (C) remove oxygen produced during respiration.   Ⓒ

    (D) supply water needed for respiration.   Ⓓ

Items 2–3 refer to the diagram below, which shows the human respiratory system.

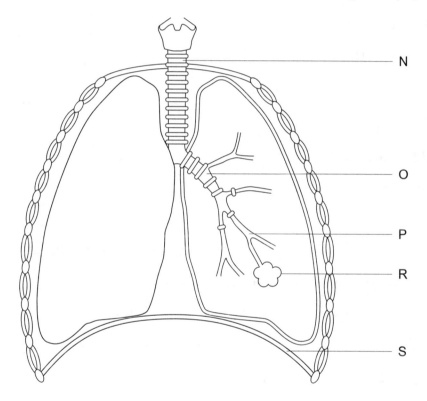

2 Structure P is

    (A) a bronchiole.   Ⓐ

    (B) a bronchus.   Ⓑ

    (C) the trachea.   Ⓒ

    (D) the larynx.   Ⓓ

3 Which labelled structure is the site of gaseous exchange?

(A) N   Ⓐ

(B) O   Ⓑ

(C) R   Ⓒ

(D) S   Ⓓ

4 Which of the following movements result in inhalation?

    I External intercostal muscles relax

    II Ribcage moves downwards and inwards

    III Diaphragm flattens

    IV Volume of thorax increases

(A) I and II only   Ⓐ

(B) I and III only   Ⓑ

(C) II and IV only   Ⓒ

(D) III and IV only   Ⓓ

5 Which sequence below correctly shows the pathway taken by inhaled air?

(A) alveoli ⟶ bronchioles ⟶ bronchi ⟶ trachea   Ⓐ

(B) trachea ⟶ bronchi ⟶ bronchioles ⟶ alveoli   Ⓑ

(C) trachea ⟶ bronchi ⟶ alveoli ⟶ bronchioles   Ⓒ

(D) bronchi ⟶ bronchioles ⟶ trachea ⟶ alveoli   Ⓓ

Item 6 refers to the following diagram, which shows some cells from the lining of the trachea.

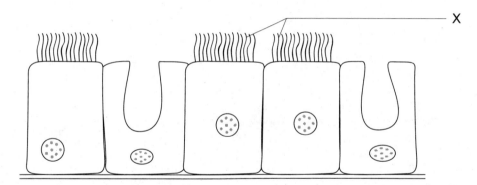

6 Which structures are labelled X?

(A) cilia   Ⓐ

(B) mucus   Ⓑ

(C) cartilage   Ⓒ

(D) flagella   Ⓓ

7 Which of the following factors will cause an increase in the breathing rate?

    I high altitude

    II sleep

    III anxiety

(A) I only   Ⓐ

(B) I and II only   Ⓑ

(C) I and III only   Ⓒ

(D) II and III only   Ⓓ

8 What is meant by the term 'vital capacity'?

(A) The maximum volume of air that can be inhaled.   Ⓐ

(B) The maximum volume of air that the lungs can contain.   Ⓑ

(C) The volume of air inhaled and exhaled while breathing normally.   Ⓒ

(D) The maximum volume of air that can be exhaled after a maximum inhalation.   Ⓓ

Items 9–10 refer to the diagram below of a section through an alveolus and a blood capillary.

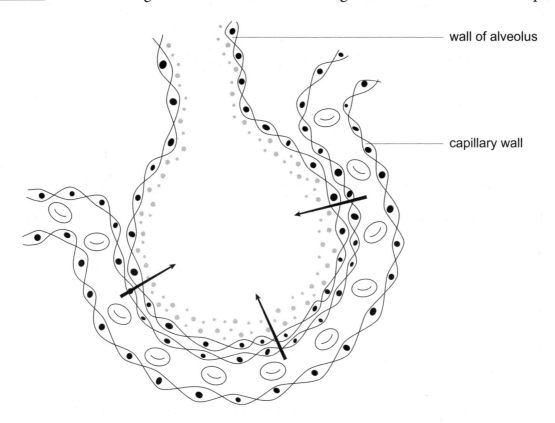

wall of alveolus

capillary wall

9 Which substance moves in the direction shown by the arrows?

(A) lymph   Ⓐ

(B) water   Ⓑ

(C) oxygen   Ⓒ

(D) carbon dioxide   Ⓓ

10 By which process does the substance move in the direction shown by the arrows?

(A) osmosis   Ⓐ

(B) diffusion   Ⓑ

(C) active transport   Ⓒ

(D) bronchial contraction   Ⓓ

11 Which of the following characteristics are common to ALL gaseous exchange surfaces?

    I moist

    II impermeable

    III large surface area

    IV thin

(A) I and II only   Ⓐ

(B) I, II and III only   Ⓑ

(C) I, III and IV only   Ⓒ

(D) I, II, III and IV   Ⓓ

12 Which word equation below correctly summarises the process of aerobic respiration?

(A) glucose + oxygen $\longrightarrow$ carbon dioxide + water + energy   Ⓐ

(B) glucose + carbon dioxide $\longrightarrow$ oxygen + water + energy   Ⓑ

(C) carbon dioxide + water + energy $\longrightarrow$ glucose + oxygen   Ⓒ

(D) glucose $\longrightarrow$ ethanol + carbon dioxide + energy   Ⓓ

13 When anaerobic respiration takes place in muscle cells, the waste product(s) is/are

(A) oxygen.   Ⓐ

(B) lactic acid.   Ⓑ

(C) carbon dioxide and ethanol.   Ⓒ

(D) carbon dioxide and lactic acid.   Ⓓ

14 Oxygen needed to convert lactic acid to carbon dioxide, water and energy following vigorous exercise is referred to as the

(A) oxygen limit.   Ⓐ

(B) oxygen debt.   Ⓑ

(C) fatigue limit.   Ⓒ

(D) breathing rate.   Ⓓ

15 Which of the following options comparing aerobic and anaerobic respiration is INCORRECT?

	Aerobic respiration	Anaerobic respiration	
(A)	takes place in the mitochondria	takes place in the cytoplasm	Ⓐ
(B)	requires oxygen	does not require oxygen	Ⓑ
(C)	produces a small amount of energy	produces a large amount of energy	Ⓒ
(D)	always produces carbon dioxide	produces carbon dioxide in some organisms	Ⓓ

16 Which of the following is described as 'the energy currency of cells'?

(A) ADH   Ⓐ

(B) ADP   Ⓑ

(C) ATP   Ⓒ

(D) DNA   Ⓓ

17 Some of the steps in mouth-to-mouth resuscitation are outlined below. Which option shows the steps in the CORRECT sequence in which they should be carried out?

   I Check that the person's chest is rising and falling.

   II Place the injured person on his/her back.

   III Cover the person's mouth completely with yours and exhale.

   IV Tilt the head backwards, open the mouth and use fingers to remove obstructions.

(A) I ⟶ II ⟶ III ⟶ IV   Ⓐ

(B) II ⟶ IV ⟶ III ⟶ I   Ⓑ

(C) II ⟶ IV ⟶ I ⟶ III   Ⓒ

(D) III ⟶ II ⟶ IV ⟶ I   Ⓓ

Items 18–19 refer to the following options.

    (A) tar   Ⓐ

    (B) nicotine   Ⓑ

    (C) carbon monoxide   Ⓒ

    (D) oxides of nitrogen   Ⓓ

Use the options above to answer EACH item. Each option may be used once, more than once or not at all.

18 The addictive substance in tobacco is

    (A)   Ⓐ

    (B)   Ⓑ

    (C)   Ⓒ

    (D)   Ⓓ

19 The component of cigarette smoke which reduces the oxygen-carrying capacity of blood is

    (A)   Ⓐ

    (B)   Ⓑ

    (C)   Ⓒ

    (D)   Ⓓ

Item 20 refers to the table below, which shows the number of smoking-related deaths in selected Caribbean countries in 2010.

Country	Number of male deaths	Number of female deaths
Barbados	64	37
Guyana	329	195
Jamaica	1119	379
Trinidad and Tobago	925	148

20 In which country was there the greatest difference between male and female smoking-related deaths in 2010?

(A) Barbados   Ⓐ

(B) Guyana   Ⓑ

(C) Jamaica   Ⓒ

(D) Trinidad and Tobago   Ⓓ

B4: The circulatory system

1 Which of the following statements explains why the human body needs a transport system?

(A) Simple diffusion is efficient enough to transport substances all around the body.   Ⓐ

(B) The human body has a small surface area to volume ratio.   Ⓑ

(C) The human body has a large surface area to volume ratio.   Ⓒ

(D) Transport distances around the human body are short.   Ⓓ

2 Materials transported around the human body include

    I urea.

    II heat.

    III hormones.

    IV carbon dioxide.

  (A) I, II and III only   (A)

  (B) II, III and IV only   (B)

  (C) I, III and IV only   (C)

  (D) I, II, III and IV   (D)

Items 3–5 refer to the following diagram of a section of the human heart.

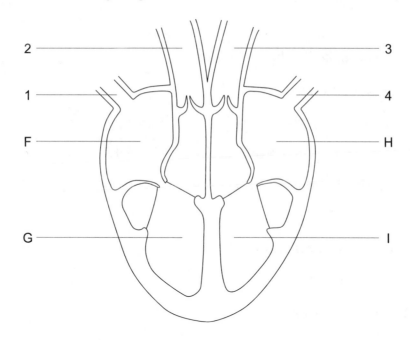

3 Which blood vessels carry deoxygenated blood?

  (A) 1 and 2   (A)

  (B) 2 and 3   (B)

  (C) 1 and 3   (C)

  (D) 3 and 4   (D)

4 The chamber labelled G is the

    (**A**) left atrium.   Ⓐ

    (**B**) left ventricle.   Ⓑ

    (**C**) right atrium.   Ⓒ

    (**D**) right ventricle.   Ⓓ

5 In which chamber of the heart is the pacemaker located?

    (**A**) F   Ⓐ

    (**B**) G   Ⓑ

    (**C**) H   Ⓒ

    (**D**) I   Ⓓ

6 The role of the pacemaker in the heart is to

    (**A**) pump blood around the body.   Ⓐ

    (**B**) regulate the breathing rate.   Ⓑ

    (**C**) prevent electrical impulses from reaching the heart.   Ⓒ

    (**D**) generate electrical impulses that cause the heart to beat.   Ⓓ

7 The role of valves in the heart is to

    (**A**) regulate the heart beat.   Ⓐ

    (**B**) reduce the blood pressure.   Ⓑ

    (**C**) prevent back flow of blood.   Ⓒ

    (**D**) cause contraction of the chambers.   Ⓓ

8 In which chamber of the heart would the blood pressure be HIGHEST?

(A) left atrium   (A)

(B) left ventricle   (B)

(C) right atrium   (C)

(D) right ventricle   (D)

9 Normal blood pressure is recorded as 120/80 mmHg. What does the figure 120 represent?

(A) pressure when the atria relax   (A)

(B) pressure when the atria contract   (B)

(C) pressure when the ventricles relax   (C)

(D) pressure when the ventricles contract   (D)

10 Contraction of the upper chambers of the heart is called

(A) atrial systole.   (A)

(B) atrial diastole.   (B)

(C) ventricular systole.   (C)

(D) ventricular diastole.   (D)

11 Which pathway below CORRECTLY shows the systemic circulation of blood?

(A) heart ⟶ lungs ⟶ heart   (A)

(B) heart ⟶ rest of the body ⟶ heart   (B)

(C) heart ⟶ lungs ⟶ rest of the body ⟶ heart   (C)

(D) heart ⟶ rest of the body ⟶ lungs ⟶ heart   (D)

12 During one complete circuit around the body, the blood flows through the heart

(A) once.   (A)

(B) twice.   (B)

(C) three times.   (C)

(D) four times.   (D)

13 The liquid component of blood, which contains water, nutrients, waste products and blood clotting factors, is called

(A) tissue fluid.   Ⓐ

(B) fibrinogen.   Ⓑ

(C) plasma.   Ⓒ

(D) serum.   Ⓓ

14 Which of the following comparisons between arteries and veins is INCORRECT?

	Arteries	Veins	
(A)	have thick walls	have thin walls	Ⓐ
(B)	valves are present	valves are absent	Ⓑ
(C)	carry blood under high pressure	carry blood under low pressure	Ⓒ
(D)	most carry oxygenated blood	most carry deoxygenated blood	Ⓓ

Items 15–17 refer to the following diagram which shows cells found in human blood.

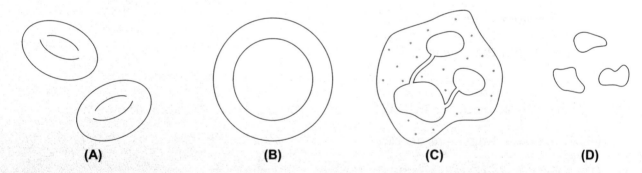

    (A)   (B)   (C)   (D)

15 Which cell transports oxygen around the body?

(A)   Ⓐ

(B)   Ⓑ

(C)   Ⓒ

(D)   Ⓓ

16 Which cell moves by using pseudopodia and engulfs bacteria?

(A)   Ⓐ

(B)   Ⓑ

(C)   Ⓒ

(D)   Ⓓ

17 Which cell produces antibodies and antitoxins?

(A)   Ⓐ

(B)   Ⓑ

(C)   Ⓒ

(D)   Ⓓ

18 Which of the following statements about red blood cells are TRUE?

    I They are the most numerous of all blood cells.

    II They contain nuclei and other organelles.

    III They are made in red bone marrow.

    IV They live for 6 to 8 months.

(A) I and II only   Ⓐ

(B) I and III only   Ⓑ

(C) II and III only   Ⓒ

(D) III and IV only   Ⓓ

19 The stages in the clotting of blood are listed below. Which option shows the stages in the CORRECT sequence?

1 Prothrombin is converted to thrombin.

2 Red blood cells are trapped by fibres.

3 Platelets release thromboplastin.

4 Fibrinogen is converted to fibrin.

(A) $3 \longrightarrow 4 \longrightarrow 1 \longrightarrow 2$ Ⓐ

(B) $3 \longrightarrow 1 \longrightarrow 4 \longrightarrow 2$ Ⓑ

(C) $1 \longrightarrow 3 \longrightarrow 2 \longrightarrow 4$ Ⓒ

(D) $4 \longrightarrow 3 \longrightarrow 2 \longrightarrow 1$ Ⓓ

20 Which vitamin plays a role in the clotting of blood?

(A) vitamin A   Ⓐ

(B) vitamin B_1 Ⓑ

(C) vitamin D   Ⓒ

(D) vitamin K   Ⓓ

21 Another name for a heart attack is

(A) angina.   Ⓐ

(B) atherosclerosis.   Ⓑ

(C) myocardial infarction.   Ⓒ

(D) pulmonary thrombosis.   Ⓓ

Items 22–23 refer to the graph below, which shows cardiovascular disease (CVD) deaths per 100 000 population for St Lucia between 2009 and 2013.

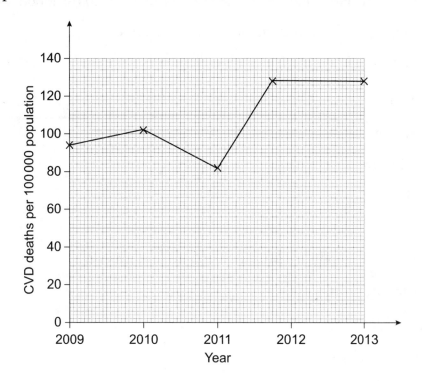

22 How many CVD deaths per 100 000 population were recorded in St Lucia in 2009?

(A) 80   Ⓐ

(B) 87   Ⓑ

(C) 94   Ⓒ

(D) 100   Ⓓ

23 Which of the following factors contributes to CVD?

(A) a high-cholesterol diet   Ⓐ

(B) low blood pressure   Ⓑ

(C) a low-sodium diet   Ⓒ

(D) regular exercise   Ⓓ

24 Which of the following are functions of the lymphatic system?

      I to transport fatty acids from the villi in the ileum to the blood

     II to supply excess fluid to tissue spaces between cells

    III to destroy microorganisms in lymph glands

(A) I and II only   Ⓐ

(B) I and III only   Ⓑ

(C) II and III only   Ⓒ

(D) I, II and III   Ⓓ

25 Where in the human body are MOST lymph nodes located?

(A) neck, armpits, groin   Ⓐ

(B) neck, shoulders, legs   Ⓑ

(C) armpits, groin, legs   Ⓒ

(D) neck, shoulders, groin   Ⓓ

26 Which fluid fills the spaces between body cells?

(A) blood   Ⓐ

(B) lymph   Ⓑ

(C) plasma   Ⓒ

(D) tissue fluid   Ⓓ

B5: The skeletal system

1 Which of the bones listed below are parts of the appendicular skeleton?

    I scapula

    II sternum

    III tibia

(A) I and II only   Ⓐ

(B) II and III only   Ⓑ

(C) I and III only   Ⓒ

(D) I, II and III   Ⓓ

2 The axial skeleton consists of the

(A) girdles, ribs, sternum.   Ⓐ

(B) girdles, forelimbs, hindlimbs.   Ⓑ

(C) skull, vertebral column, girdles, ribs.   Ⓒ

(D) skull, vertebral column, ribs, sternum.   Ⓓ

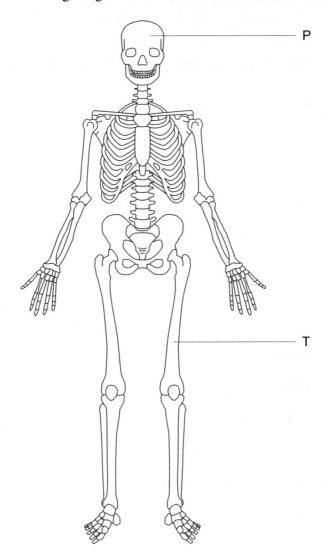

3 Which bone is labelled T?

(A) femur

(B) sacrum

(C) humerus

(D) clavicle

(A)

(B)

(C)

(D)

4 Which type of joint holds the bones of the structure labelled P together?

(A) hinge   Ⓐ

(B) fixed   Ⓑ

(C) cartilaginous   Ⓒ

(D) ball and socket   Ⓓ

Items 5–6 refer to the diagram below which shows a section of a human bone.

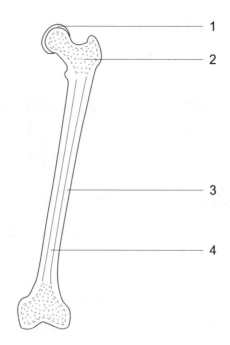

5 Which labelled part contributes MOST to the strength of bone?

(A) 1   Ⓐ

(B) 2   Ⓑ

(C) 3   Ⓒ

(D) 4   Ⓓ

6 The part labelled 2

      I is compact bone.

     II produces white blood cells.

    III contains red bone marrow.

(A) I and II only   Ⓐ

(B) II and III only   Ⓑ

(C) I and III only   Ⓒ

(D) I, II and III   Ⓓ

7 Which of the following is a feature of cartilage, but NOT of bone?

(A) It is flexible.   Ⓐ

(B) It contains protein.   Ⓑ

(C) It contains calcium salts.   Ⓒ

(D) It contains living cells.   Ⓓ

8 Cartilage is important as it

(A) connects one bone to another.   Ⓐ

(B) connects muscles to bones.   Ⓑ

(C) lubricates the joints.   Ⓒ

(D) is a shock absorber.   Ⓓ

9 Which option in the table below CORRECTLY identifies a feature and a function of tendons and ligaments?

	Tendons	Ligaments	
(A)	are elastic; join bone to bone	are non-elastic; join bone to bone	Ⓐ
(B)	are elastic; join muscle to bone	are non-elastic; join muscle to bone	Ⓑ
(C)	are non-elastic; join bone to bone	are elastic; join muscle to bone	Ⓒ
(D)	are non-elastic; join muscle to bone	are elastic; join bone to bone	Ⓓ

Items 10–11 refer to the following diagram of a section through a joint.

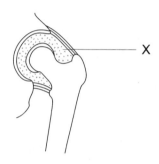

10 Which statement about the joint is CORRECT?

(**A**) It is a fixed joint.   Ⓐ

(**B**) It allows movement in one plane.   Ⓑ

(**C**) It is a partially moveable joint.   Ⓒ

(**D**) It allows movement in all planes.   Ⓓ

11 What is the function of the part labelled X?

(**A**) to lubricate the joint   Ⓐ

(**B**) to secrete synovial fluid   Ⓑ

(**C**) to hold the bones together   Ⓒ

(**D**) to increase friction between bones   Ⓓ

12 Which type of joint is found at the knee?

(A) fixed   (A)

(B) hinge   (B)

(C) ball and socket   (C)

(D) partially moveable   (D)

13 'The attachment point of the muscle to a bone that moves when the muscle contracts' describes the

(A) origin of a muscle.   (A)

(B) insertion of a muscle.   (B)

(C) flexor muscle.   (C)

(D) extensor muscle.   (D)

14 Muscles that work in opposition to cause movement at a joint are described as

(A) opposite.   (A)

(B) automatic.   (B)

(C) pentadactyl.   (C)

(D) antagonistic.   (D)

15 The flexor muscle of the upper arm

(A) relaxes to bend the elbow joint.   (A)

(B) contracts to straighten the elbow joint.   (B)

(C) contracts to bend the elbow joint.   (C)

(D) relaxes to straighten the elbow joint.   (D)

16 Which option in the table below is correct for when the human elbow is straightened?

	Biceps	Triceps	
(A)	contracts	contracts	Ⓐ
(B)	contracts	relaxes	Ⓑ
(C)	relaxes	relaxes	Ⓒ
(D)	relaxes	contracts	Ⓓ

17 Which of the following is NOT an effect of exercise on muscles and joints?

(A) muscles become larger   Ⓐ

(B) muscle tone is reduced   Ⓑ

(C) joints become more flexible   Ⓒ

(D) more capillaries are produced in muscles   Ⓓ

18 Which of the following are reasons locomotion is important to humans?

    I to search for a mate

    II to search for food

    III to avoid danger

    IV to avoid new habitats

(A) I and II only   Ⓐ

(B) II and III only   Ⓑ

(C) I, II and III only   Ⓒ

(D) I, II, III and IV   Ⓓ

19 Cara is described as having bad posture. Which of the following may occur as a result of her posture?

     I fatigue and backache

    II more efficient digestion

   III less efficient breathing

   IV compressed blood vessels

(A) I and III only   Ⓐ

(B) I, II and IV only   Ⓑ

(C) I, III and IV only   Ⓒ

(D) I, II, III and IV   Ⓓ

B6: Excretion and homeostasis

1 Excretion may be defined as

(A) the loss of water and salts through sweat.   Ⓐ

(B) the production of metabolic waste in the body.   Ⓑ

(C) the removal of metabolic waste from the body.   Ⓒ

(D) the removal of undigested food from the body.   Ⓓ

2 Metabolic waste does NOT include

(A) urea.   Ⓐ

(B) faeces.   Ⓑ

(C) salts.   Ⓒ

(D) carbon dioxide.   Ⓓ

3 Which of the following is/are reason(s) excretion is important to humans?

    I Waste products can damage and kill body cells.

    II Excretion helps to keep the internal environment constant.

    III Excretion helps in the breakdown of food in the body.

(A) I only   Ⓐ

(B) I and II only   Ⓑ

(C) I and III only   Ⓒ

(D) II and III only   Ⓓ

4 Which option in the table below CORRECTLY matches the excretory organ(s) and the waste excreted?

	Organ(s)	Waste excreted	
(A)	skin	carbon dioxide, water, salts	Ⓐ
(B)	lungs	water, urea, salts	Ⓑ
(C)	kidneys	bile pigments, water, urea	Ⓒ
(D)	liver	bile pigments	Ⓓ

Items 5–6 refer to the diagram below which shows the human urinary system.

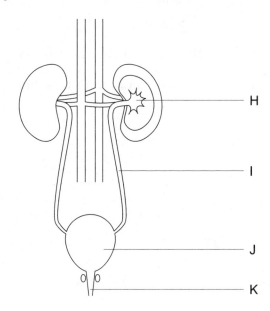

5 Which option in the table below correctly identifies H, I and K?

	H	I	K	
(A)	pelvis	ureter	urethra	Ⓐ
(B)	cortex	urethra	ureter	Ⓑ
(C)	medulla	ureter	urethra	Ⓒ
(D)	pelvis	urethra	ureter	Ⓓ

6 The function of the structure labelled J is to

(A) filter blood.   Ⓐ

(B) produce urine.   Ⓑ

(C) store urine.   Ⓒ

(D) carry urine out of the body.   Ⓓ

Item 7 refers to the following diagram of a nephron.

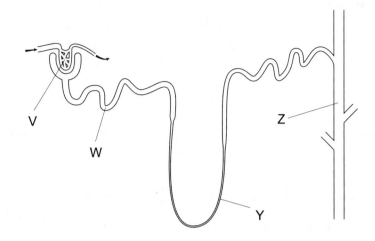

7 In which labelled region of the nephron does ultrafiltration take place?

(A) V   Ⓐ

(B) W   Ⓑ

(C) Y   Ⓒ

(D) Z   Ⓓ

8 Which of the following substances are normally found in the filtrate formed by ultrafiltration?

    I   vitamins

    II   glucose

    III   amino acids

    IV   red blood cells

(A) I, II and III only   Ⓐ

(B) II and III only   Ⓑ

(C) II, III and IV only   Ⓒ

(D) I, II, III and IV   Ⓓ

9 All of the following substances would be present in the blood plasma, filtrate AND urine of a healthy individual EXCEPT

(A) urea. Ⓐ

(B) water. Ⓑ

(C) glucose. Ⓒ

(D) mineral salts. Ⓓ

10 In what way is a kidney dialysis machine similar to a healthy kidney?

(A) It breaks down amino acids to urea. Ⓐ

(B) It removes sugar from the blood. Ⓑ

(C) It removes large proteins from the blood. Ⓒ

(D) It regulates the concentration of the blood. Ⓓ

Items 11–13 refer to the following simplified diagram of the human skin.

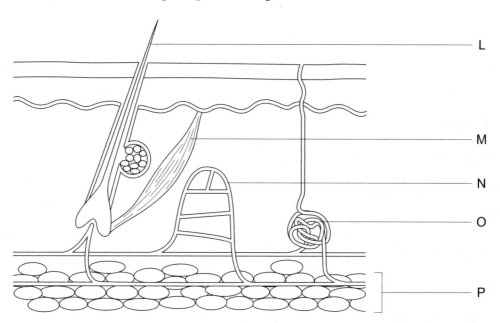

11 What is the structure labelled O?

(A) fat cell Ⓐ

(B) hair follicle Ⓑ

(C) blood vessel Ⓒ

(D) sweat gland Ⓓ

12 The function(s) of the layer labelled P include(s)

      I protecting the body against ultraviolet radiation from the Sun

    II helping to protect the body against damage

   III acting as insulation

(A) I only   (A)

(B) II only   (B)

(C) II and III only   (C)

(D) I, II and III   (D)

13 On a very cold day

(A) part L will lie flat.   (A)

(B) part M will relax.   (B)

(C) part N will constrict.   (C)

(D) secretions from part O will increase. (D)

14 Which of the following is kept constant by a homeostatic mechanism in the body?

(A) heart rate   (A)

(B) breathing rate   (B)

(C) volume of urine excreted   (C)

(D) water content of the blood   (D)

15 'A system in which a change from the normal condition is detected and a response is given which restores the normal condition' defines a

(A) positive feedback mechanism.   (A)

(B) negative feedback mechanism. (B)

(C) self-regulation mechanism.   (C)

(D) external mechanism.   (D)

16 Which option below shows the role of the hormone insulin CORRECTLY matched with its effect on blood glucose concentration?

	Role of insulin	Blood glucose concentration
(A)	glycogen $\longrightarrow$ glucose	increases
(B)	glycogen $\longrightarrow$ glucose	decreases
(C)	glucose $\longrightarrow$ glycogen	increases
(D)	glucose $\longrightarrow$ glycogen	decreases

Ⓐ
Ⓑ
Ⓒ
Ⓓ

17 Antidiuretic hormone causes the kidneys to

(A) reabsorb less water from the filtrate. Ⓐ

(B) reabsorb more water from the filtrate. Ⓑ

(C) pass out more water. Ⓒ

(D) reabsorb more salts from the filtrate. Ⓓ

18 Which of the following factors will cause the body to release large amounts of dilute urine?

    I exercise

    II cold weather

    III eating salty foods

    IV drinking a lot of water

(A) I and II only Ⓐ

(B) I and III only Ⓑ

(C) II and IV only Ⓒ

(D) III and IV only Ⓓ

19 Which statement below about heat or temperature is CORRECT?

(A) Heat is measured in joules. Ⓐ

(B) Temperature is a form of energy. Ⓑ

(C) Temperature is measured using a barometer. Ⓒ

(D) Heat is a measure of how hot or cold something is. Ⓓ

20 What is considered to be the normal human body temperature?

(A) 25 °C   (A)

(B) 37 °C   (B)

(C) 42 °C   (C)

(D) 98.6 °C   (D)

B7: Coordination and control

Items 1–2 refer to the tree diagram below of the human nervous system.

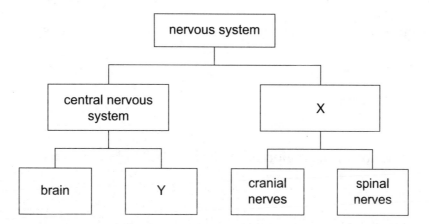

1 X represents the

(A) spinal cord.   (A)

(B) sense organs.   (B)

(C) automatic nervous system.   (C)

(D) peripheral nervous system.   (D)

2 What does Y represent?

(A) a receptor   (A)

(B) an effector   (B)

(C) the spinal cord   (C)

(D) a sensory neurone   (D)

Items 3-4 refer to the diagram of the human brain below.

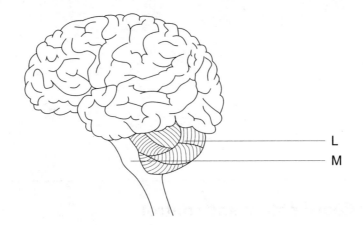

3 L is the

(A) cerebellum.　　　　　　　　　　　　　　　　　　　Ⓐ

(B) cerebrum.　　　　　　　　　　　　　　　　　　　Ⓑ

(C) spinal cord.　　　　　　　　　　　　　　　　　　Ⓒ

(D) medulla oblongata.　　　　　　　　　　　　　　　Ⓓ

4 What is the function of the region of the brain labelled M?

(A) controls balance and posture　　　　　　　　　　　Ⓐ

(B) controls conscious thoughts and emotions　　　　　　Ⓑ

(C) controls heart rate and breathing rate　　　　　　　Ⓒ

(D) releases hormones involved in growth and reproduction　Ⓓ

5 Which part of the brain monitors the internal environment and controls water balance and temperature?

(A) pituitary gland　　　　　　　　　　　　　　　　Ⓐ

(B) hypothalamus　　　　　　　　　　　　　　　　　Ⓑ

(C) cerebellum　　　　　　　　　　　　　　　　　　Ⓒ

(D) cerebrum　　　　　　　　　　　　　　　　　　　Ⓓ

6 'A bundle of nerve fibres surrounded by connective tissue' describes a

(A) nerve. Ⓐ

(B) neurone. Ⓑ

(C) receptor. Ⓒ

(D) reflex bundle. Ⓓ

Items 7–8 refer to the following diagram of a nerve cell.

7 The nerve cell shown transmits impulses

(A) throughout the central nervous system. Ⓐ

(B) from receptors to the central nervous system. Ⓑ

(C) from the central nervous system to effectors. Ⓒ

(D) from effectors to the central nervous system. Ⓓ

8 Which labelled structure is the axon?

(A) Q Ⓐ

(B) R Ⓑ

(C) S Ⓒ

(D) T Ⓓ

9 The chemical that carries a nervous impulse across a synapse is

(A) an enzyme.   Ⓐ

(B) a hormone.   Ⓑ

(C) synaptic fluid.   Ⓒ

(D) a neurotransmitter.   Ⓓ

10 Which of the following is a function of synapses?

(A) to detect stimuli   Ⓐ

(B) to respond to stimuli   Ⓑ

(C) to help impulses to travel in many directions   Ⓒ

(D) to ensure impulses travel in one direction only   Ⓓ

11 Which of the following statements about reflex actions is/are INCORRECT?

    I They are rapid.

    II They are learned.

    III They are voluntary.

(A) II only   Ⓐ

(B) II and III only   Ⓑ

(C) I and III only   Ⓒ

(D) III only   Ⓓ

Items 12–13 refer to the following diagram of a reflex arc.

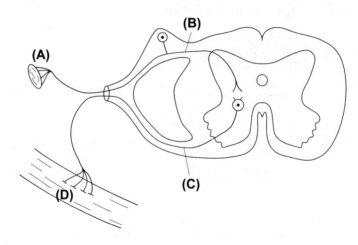

Match each item below to one of the options above, each of which may be used once, more than once or not at all.

12 Carries messages to the central nervous system.

   (A)   Ⓐ

   (B)   Ⓑ

   (C)   Ⓒ

   (D)   Ⓓ

13 Detects a stimulus.

   (A)   Ⓐ

   (B)   Ⓑ

   (C)   Ⓒ

   (D)   Ⓓ

14 When an object approaches his eyes rapidly, Diego blinks. Which option shows the receptor(s) and effectors for this reflex action?

	Receptor(s)	Effectors
(A)	cells of the retina	eyelid muscles
(B)	cornea	eyelid muscles
(C)	cells of the retina	ciliary muscles
(D)	pupil	ciliary muscles

(A)
(B)
(C)
(D)

15 Which of the following is an example of a voluntary action?

(A) sneezing   Ⓐ

(B) saliva production   Ⓑ

(C) waving to a friend   Ⓒ

(D) dropping a hot plate   Ⓓ

16 Which of the following statements is/are CORRECT?

    I Voluntary actions involve the cerebrum.

    II Involuntary actions involve complex pathways.

    III Voluntary actions do not involve the spinal cord.

    IV Involuntary actions do not involve the brain.

(A) I only   Ⓐ

(B) I and II only   Ⓑ

(C) II and III only   Ⓒ

(D) III and IV only   Ⓓ

17 Which option below INCORRECTLY matches the sense organ and the stimulus it detects?

	Sense organ	Stimulus	
(A)	ear	sound	Ⓐ
(B)	eye	light	Ⓑ
(C)	skin	gravity	Ⓒ
(D)	tongue	chemicals	Ⓓ

Items 18–20 refer to the diagram below, which shows a section of the human eye.

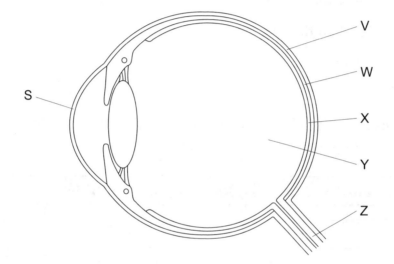

18 Y is the

(A) cornea.   Ⓐ

(B) retina.   Ⓑ

(C) aqueous humour.   Ⓒ

(D) vitreous humour.   Ⓓ

19 What is the function of the part of the eye labelled S?

(A) refracts light rays   Ⓐ

(B) prevents internal reflection   Ⓑ

(C) changes the shape of the lens   Ⓒ

(D) controls the amount of light entering the eye   Ⓓ

20 Which region of the eye contains light-sensitive cells?

(A) V   Ⓐ

(B) W   Ⓑ

(C) X   Ⓒ

(D) Z   Ⓓ

21 Which option correctly describes the image that is formed on the retina of the eye?

(A) inverted, larger than the object   Ⓐ

(B) inverted, smaller than the object   Ⓑ

(C) upright, larger than the object   Ⓒ

(D) upright, smaller than the object   Ⓓ

22 A person walks from a brightly lit room into a dark room. How do the muscles of the iris and the pupil respond to this change in light intensity?

	Circular muscles of the iris	Radial muscles of the iris	Pupil	
(A)	relax	contract	constricts	Ⓐ
(B)	contract	relax	constricts	Ⓑ
(C)	relax	contract	dilates	Ⓒ
(D)	contract	relax	dilates	Ⓓ

Item 23 refers to the diagram below, which shows simplified sections through the human eye, each adapted to view objects at different distances from the eye.

(A)   (B)   (C)   (D)

23 Which figure shows accommodation to view the nearest object?

(A)   Ⓐ

(B)   Ⓑ

(C)   Ⓒ

(D)   Ⓓ

Items 24–25 refers to the diagram below, which shows a section through an eye with a sight defect.

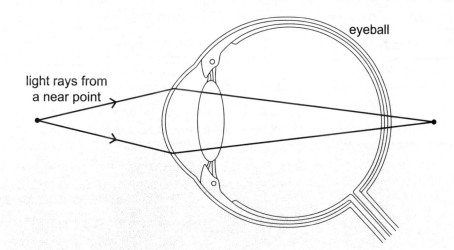

eyeball

light rays from a near point

24 Which sight defect is shown?

(A) short-sightedness   Ⓐ

(B) long-sightedness   Ⓑ

(C) astigmatism   Ⓒ

(D) glaucoma   Ⓓ

25 Which of the lenses shown below could be used to correct the sight defect shown?

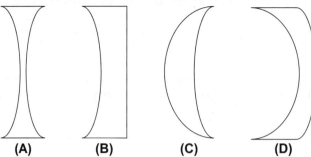

(A)　(B)　(C)　(D)

(A)
(B)
(C)
(D)

26 Which eye condition occurs when the lens becomes opaque?

(A) cataract

(B) glaucoma

(C) presbyopia

(D) astigmatism

(A)
(B)
(C)
(D)

27 Which comparison between endocrine and nervous control systems is INCORRECT?

	Endocrine system	Nervous system
(A)	uses hormones	uses nerve impulses
(B)	effects are widespread	effects are localised
(C)	responses are long-lasting	responses are short-lived
(D)	transmission is rapid	transmission is relatively slow

(A)
(B)
(C)
(D)

Items 28–29 refer to the diagram below which shows the positions of the main endocrine glands in the human body.

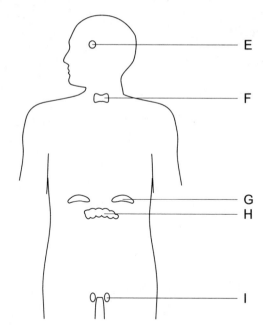

28 The hormone that prepares the body for fight or flight is produced in

(A) E

(B) F

(C) G

(D) H

    (A)

    (B)

    (C)

    (D)

29 Which endocrine gland secretes the main hormones involved in regulating the blood glucose level?

(A) F

(B) G

(C) H

(D) I

    (A)

    (B)

    (C)

    (D)

30 The pituitary gland produces all of the following hormones, EXCEPT

   I thyroxine.

   II growth hormone.

   III anti-diuretic hormone.

   IV follicle-stimulating hormone.

(A) I only Ⓐ

(B) I and II only Ⓑ

(C) II and III only Ⓒ

(D) IV only Ⓓ

31 Which hormone is responsible for controlling sperm production?

(A) glucagon Ⓐ

(B) adrenaline Ⓑ

(C) progesterone Ⓒ

(D) testosterone Ⓓ

B8: The reproductive system

1 Which of the following comparisons between sexual and asexual reproduction is INCORRECT?

	Sexual reproduction	Asexual reproduction	
(A)	involves two parents	involves one parent	Ⓐ
(B)	involves mitosis	involves meiosis	Ⓑ
(C)	the process is slow	the process is rapid	Ⓒ
(D)	produces variation among offspring	produces genetically identical offspring	Ⓓ

Item 2 refers to the following diagram of the female reproductive system.

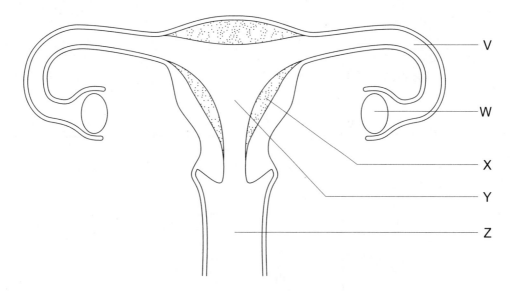

2 In which of the labelled regions do fertilisation and implantation normally take place?

	Fertilisation	Implantation
(A)	V	X
(B)	V	Y
(C)	Z	Y
(D)	W	X

(A)
(B)
(C)
(D)

Items 3–4 refer to the following diagram of the male reproductive system.

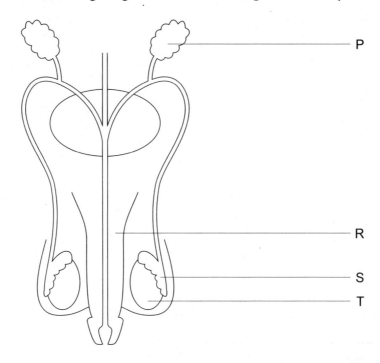

3 Which structure produces the male gametes?

(A) P   Ⓐ

(B) R   Ⓑ

(C) S   Ⓒ

(D) T   Ⓓ

4 What is the function of the structure labelled P?

(A) sperm production   Ⓐ

(B) storage of sperm   Ⓑ

(C) to add fluid secretions to sperm   Ⓒ

(D) production of male sex hormones   Ⓓ

5 Which of the following statements about sperm cells is/are CORRECT?

     I They are produced from birth.

     II They swim using tails.

     III They can live for 2–3 days in the female body.

(A) I and II only   Ⓐ

(B) I and III only   Ⓑ

(C) II only   Ⓒ

(D) II and III only   Ⓓ

6 Which of the following types of cancer is usually caused by a sexually transmitted virus?

(A) breast cancer   Ⓐ

(B) cervical cancer   Ⓑ

(C) ovarian cancer   Ⓒ

(D) prostate cancer   Ⓓ

Items 7–8 refer to the diagram below, which shows changes to the uterus lining during the menstrual cycle.

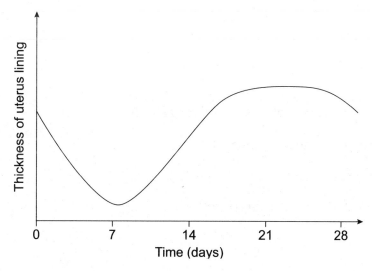

7 The process that is MOST likely to occur between days 1 and 7 is

(A) ovulation.   Ⓐ

(B) ejaculation.   Ⓑ

(C) fertilisation.   Ⓒ

(D) menstruation.   Ⓓ

8 Which hormone is responsible for the thickening of the uterus lining between days 7 and 14?

(A) oestrogen   Ⓐ

(B) progesterone   Ⓑ

(C) luteinising hormone   Ⓒ

(D) follicle-stimulating hormone   Ⓓ

9 Which hormone is INCORRECTLY matched with the structure that secretes it?

	Hormone	Secreted by the	
(A)	oestrogen	Graafian follicle	Ⓐ
(B)	progesterone	corpus luteum	Ⓑ
(C)	luteinising hormone	pituitary gland	Ⓒ
(D)	follicle-stimulating hormone	Graafian follicle	Ⓓ

10 The fusion of sperm and ovum produces a/an

(A) embryo.   Ⓐ

(B) foetus.   Ⓑ

(C) zygote.   Ⓒ

(D) placenta.   Ⓓ

11 Which of the following events take(s) place after fertilisation?

    I The progesterone level falls.

    II Another follicle matures in an ovary.

    III A ball of cells becomes implanted in the uterus lining.

(A) I only   Ⓐ

(B) III only   Ⓑ

(C) I and II only   Ⓒ

(D) II and III only   Ⓓ

12 The role of the placenta during pregnancy is to

(A) secrete oestrogen. Ⓐ

(B) support and protect the foetus. Ⓑ

(C) produce food needed by the foetus. Ⓒ

(D) exchange substances between the blood of the mother and the foetus. Ⓓ

13 What is the normal position of the baby in the uterus just before birth?

(A) head up Ⓐ

(B) head down Ⓑ

(C) horizontal Ⓒ

(D) legs down Ⓓ

14 The events listed below occur during the birth process. Which option shows these events in the order in which they occur?

1 Muscles in the uterus wall begin to contract.

2 The placenta is pushed out through the vagina.

3 The baby is pushed out through the cervix and the vagina.

4 The pituitary gland secretes oxytocin.

(A) 4 ⟶ 1 ⟶ 3 ⟶ 2 Ⓐ

(B) 1 ⟶ 3 ⟶ 2 ⟶ 4 Ⓑ

(C) 1 ⟶ 2 ⟶ 3 ⟶ 4 Ⓒ

(D) 4 ⟶ 1 ⟶ 2 ⟶ 3 Ⓓ

15 During pre-natal care, mothers are advised NOT to

(A) take vitamin supplements. Ⓐ

(B) avoid infections. Ⓑ

(C) exercise. Ⓒ

(D) smoke. Ⓓ

16 Which of the following statements is NOT true of breast milk?

(A) It is sterile. Ⓐ

(B) It contains antibodies. Ⓑ

(C) It is unaffected by the mother's diet. Ⓒ

(D) It is at the correct temperature for the baby. Ⓓ

17 Which birth control method is INCORRECTLY matched with how it works?

	Birth control method	How it works	
(A)	diaphragm	prevents sperm from reaching the ovum	Ⓐ
(B)	intra-uterine device (IUD)	prevents ovulation	Ⓑ
(C)	rhythm method	no intercourse around the time of ovulation	Ⓒ
(D)	vasectomy	sperm ducts are cut and tied off	Ⓓ

18 Which of the following are advantages of using the contraceptive pill?

I very reliable

II easy to use

III makes menstruation less painful

IV prevents sexually transmitted infections

(A) I and II only Ⓐ

(B) I, II and III only Ⓑ

(C) I, II and IV only Ⓒ

(D) II, III and IV only Ⓓ

19 Spontaneous abortions may be caused by all of the following, EXCEPT

(A) exercising daily. Ⓐ

(B) improper implantation. Ⓑ

(C) abnormal foetal development. Ⓒ

(D) excessive alcohol consumption. Ⓓ

20 Which of the following are advantages of family planning?

    I It allows parents to determine the spacing of their children.

    II It allows parents to determine the sex of their children.

    III It is less expensive to have small families.

(A) I and II only   (A)

(B) II and III only   (B)

(C) I and III only   (C)

(D) I, II and III   (D)

Section C: Heredity and variation
C1: Cell division and variation

1 How many chromosomes are found in the nucleus of a normal human body cell?

(A) 22   (A)

(B) 23   (B)

(C) 46   (C)

(D) 47   (D)

2 Which of the following statements about mitosis are TRUE?

    I It produces two daughter cells.

    II It produces four daughter cells.

    III It produces identical daughter cells.

    IV It only takes place during gamete production.

(A) I and II only   (A)

(B) I and III only   (B)

(C) II and IV only   (C)

(D) II, III and IV only   (D)

Item 3 refers to the following diagram, which shows the nucleus of an animal cell before mitosis takes place.

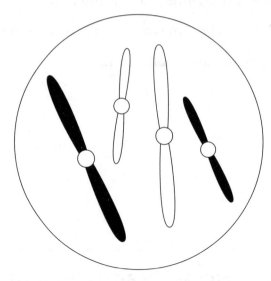

3 Which of the following options shows the nuclei that would be produced when the cell undergoes mitosis?

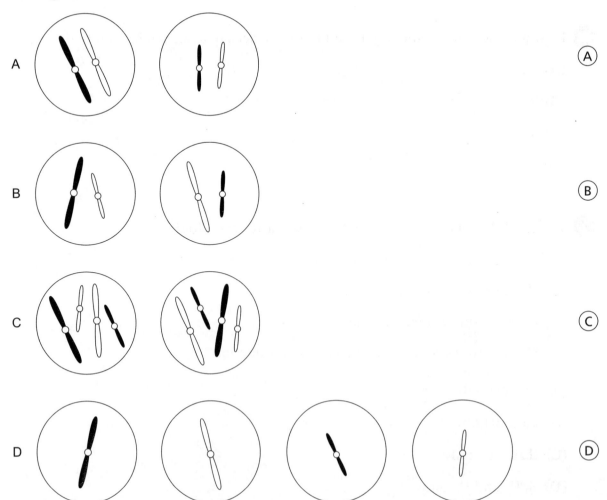

A

B

C

D

Item 4 refers to the following diagram of an animal cell undergoing mitosis.

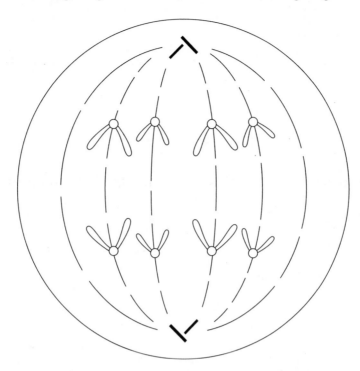

4 What is the diploid number of chromosomes for this organism?

(A) 2   Ⓐ

(B) 4   Ⓑ

(C) 8   Ⓒ

(D) 16   Ⓓ

5 Which of the following are reasons mitosis is important to living organisms?

    I for growth of organisms

    II for sexual reproduction

    III for repair of damaged tissues

    IV to maintain the species number of chromosomes

(A) I and II only   Ⓐ

(B) III and IV only   Ⓑ

(C) I, II and III only   Ⓒ

(D) I, III and IV only   Ⓓ

6 How many cell divisions take place during meiosis?

(A) 1   Ⓐ

(B) 2   Ⓑ

(C) 3   Ⓒ

(D) 4   Ⓓ

7 Pairs of chromosomes that are similar in size and genetic composition are called

(A) homologous chromosomes.   Ⓐ

(B) sister chromosomes.   Ⓑ

(C) homozygous chromosomes.   Ⓒ

(D) haploid chromosomes.   Ⓓ

8 Which of the following processes take place during meiosis?

    I pairing of homologous chromosomes

    II exchange of genetic material between chromatids

    III separation of homologous chromosomes

    IV separation of chromatids

(A) I, II and III only   Ⓐ

(B) I, II and IV only   Ⓑ

(C) II, III and IV only   Ⓒ

(D) I, II, III and IV   Ⓓ

9 In which of the following organs does meiosis take place?

(A) the liver   Ⓐ

(B) the heart   Ⓑ

(C) the ovaries   Ⓒ

(D) the kidneys   Ⓓ

10 The diploid chromosome number of a mouse is 40. How many chromosomes would be present in a sperm cell from this organism?

(A) 10   Ⓐ

(B) 20   Ⓑ

(C) 40   Ⓒ

(D) 80   Ⓓ

11 Meiosis is important to living organisms for ALL of the following reasons, EXCEPT

(A) for gamete production.   Ⓐ

(B) to contribute to variation among offspring.   Ⓑ

(C) to reduce the chromosome number of daughter cells.   Ⓒ

(D) to maintain the chromosome number of daughter cells.   Ⓓ

12 Genetic variation is important to living organisms because it

    I drives natural selection.

    II improves the chances of survival of a species.

    III ensures that favourable gene combinations are maintained.

    IV enables species to adapt to changing environmental conditions.

(A) I and II only   Ⓐ

(B) II and III only   Ⓑ

(C) I, II and IV only   Ⓒ

(D) I, II, III and IV   Ⓓ

13 Which of the following comparisons between genetic and environmental variation is INCORRECT?

	Genetic variation	Environmental variation	
(A)	occurs in populations that reproduce sexually only	occurs in populations that reproduce asexually only	Ⓐ
(B)	variation may be passed on to offspring	variation cannot be passed on to offspring	Ⓑ
(C)	affects the genotype and the phenotype	mainly affects the phenotype	Ⓒ
(D)	may be due to mutation	may be due to diet	Ⓓ

14 Which of the following traits show discontinuous variation in humans?

    I height

    II weight

    III blood group

    IV tongue rolling

(A) I and II only   Ⓐ

(B) I and III only   Ⓑ

(C) II and IV only   Ⓒ

(D) III and IV only   Ⓓ

15 'A sudden change in a single gene or in a chromosome that changes characteristics of an organism' defines

(A) a mutation.   Ⓐ

(B) a mutagen.   Ⓑ

(C) variation.   Ⓒ

(D) an adaptation.   Ⓓ

1 Genes are composed of

(A) DNA. Ⓐ

(B) proteins. Ⓑ

(C) carbohydrates. Ⓒ

(D) chromosomes. Ⓓ

2 The phenotype of an organism is defined as the

(A) genetic make-up of the organism. Ⓐ

(B) observable characteristics of the organism. Ⓑ

(C) number of chromosomes in each body cell. Ⓒ

(D) different forms of a gene an organism has. Ⓓ

3 Alternative forms of a gene are called

(A) alleles. Ⓐ

(B) genotypes. Ⓑ

(C) phenotypes. Ⓒ

(D) chromosomes. Ⓓ

4 An organism that has two alleles which are the same is referred to as

(A) dominant. Ⓐ

(B) recessive. Ⓑ

(C) homozygous. Ⓒ

(D) heterozygous. Ⓓ

5 Which of the following statements is/are TRUE about recessive alleles?

    I They always cause diseases.

    II They are not shown in the phenotype.

    III They are only shown in the phenotype when their paired alleles are the same.

(A) I only   Ⓐ

(B) II only   Ⓑ

(C) III only   Ⓒ

(D) I and II only   Ⓓ

6 Using 'A' to represent the allele for normal pigmentation and 'a' to represent the allele for albinism, what are the possible genotypes of parents who both have normal pigmentation and have an albino child?

(A) aa and aa   Ⓐ

(B) Aa and Aa   Ⓑ

(C) AA and aa   Ⓒ

(D) AA and AA   Ⓓ

7 If Hb^A represents the allele for production of normal haemoglobin A and Hb^S represents the allele for production of abnormal haemoglobin S, which of the following represents the genotype of a person who has the sickle cell trait?

(A) $Hb^A Hb^A$ Ⓐ

(B) $Hb^A Hb^S$ Ⓑ

(C) $Hb^S Hb^S$ Ⓒ

(D) Hb^S Ⓓ

8 Tongue rolling is dominant to non-tongue rolling. What is the probability of parents who are both non-tongue rollers having a child who is a tongue roller?

(A) 100%

(B) 50%

(C) 25%

(D) 0%

(A)

(B)

(C)

(D)

9 Which option in the table below correctly shows the combination of human sex chromosomes in the nuclei of body cells?

	Male	Female
(A)	XX	XY
(B)	XY	YY
(C)	XY	XX
(D)	YY	XX

(A)

(B)

(C)

(D)

10 When fertilisation takes place in humans, what is the probability of the offspring being male?

(A) 25%

(B) 50%

(C) 75%

(D) 100%

(A)

(B)

(C)

(D)

Items 11–12 refer to the following family tree which shows the inheritance of haemophilia, a sex-linked condition caused by a recessive allele, 'h', carried on the X chromosome.

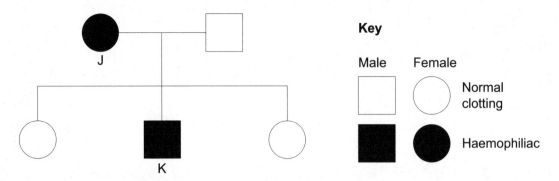

Key

Male | Female

□ ○ Normal clotting

■ ● Haemophiliac

11 What is the genotype of person J?

(A) $X^H X^H$ Ⓐ

(B) $X^H X^h$ Ⓑ

(C) $X^h X^h$ Ⓒ

(D) $X^h Y$ Ⓓ

12 If person K marries a normal female who is homozygous, what is the probability that they would have a haemophiliac son?

(A) 100%   Ⓐ

(B) 50%   Ⓑ

(C) 25%   Ⓒ

(D) 0%   Ⓓ

13 'Changing traits of one organism by inserting genetic material from another organism' defines

(A) natural selection.   Ⓐ

(B) artificial selection.   Ⓑ

(C) genetic engineering.   Ⓒ

(D) traditional breeding.   Ⓓ

14 Which of the following are ways in which genetic engineering is used?

    I To produce human clones.

    II To produce drugs and vaccines.

    III To increase the nutritional value of food.

    IV To produce high-yielding crops and animals.

(A) I and II only   Ⓐ

(B) II and III only   Ⓑ

(C) I, II and III only   Ⓒ

(D) II, III and IV only   Ⓓ

15 Which of the following is NOT a possible disadvantage of genetic engineering?

(A) Genetically modified organisms may interbreed with wild species.   Ⓐ

(B) Reduced use of chemical pesticides.   Ⓑ

(C) Long-term human health risks.   Ⓒ

(D) Increased allergens in food.   Ⓓ

Section D: Disease and its impact on humans
D1: Disease (1)

1 Which of the following are components of good health, as defined by the World Health Organization?

    I physical well-being

    II social well-being

    III access to clean water

    IV health insurance coverage

(A) I and II only   Ⓐ

(B) I, II and III only   Ⓑ

(C) I, III and IV only   Ⓒ

(D) I, II, III and IV   Ⓓ

2 Which option below shows diseases INCORRECTLY categorised as communicable or non-communicable?

	Communicable disease	Non-communicable disease	
(A)	typhoid	rickets	Ⓐ
(B)	cholera	obesity	Ⓑ
(C)	hypertension	herpes	Ⓒ
(D)	gastroenteritis	diabetes mellitus	Ⓓ

3 What does the term 'chronic' mean in reference to a disease?

(A) It has short-term effects. Ⓐ

(B) It is experienced over a long period. Ⓑ

(C) It can be cured using medication. Ⓒ

(D) It can be prevented by vaccination. Ⓓ

<u>Items 4–5</u> refer to the following options.

(A) inherited disorder

(B) infectious disease

(C) deficiency disease

(D) degenerative disease

Match EACH item below with one of the options above. Each option may be used once, more than once or not at all.

4 Caused by a breakdown of body tissues that prevents them from functioning normally.

(A) Ⓐ

(B) Ⓑ

(C) Ⓒ

(D) Ⓓ

5 Caused by a faulty gene passed from one generation to the next.

(A)   (A)

(B)   (B)

(C)   (C)

(D)   (D)

6 Which of the following are signs of a disease?

> **I** rash
>
> **II** pain
>
> **III** fatigue
>
> **IV** abnormal heart rate

(A) I and II only   (A)

(B) II and III only   (B)

(C) III and IV only   (C)

(D) I and IV only   (D)

7 Symptoms of a disease

(A) are observed by others.   (A)

(B) can be detected or measured.   (B)

(C) are what the person feels.   (C)

(D) are experienced for a short time.   (D)

8 Asthma attacks can be caused by ALL of the following, EXCEPT

(A) pollen.   (A)

(B) anxiety.   (B)

(C) exercise.   (C)

(D) low blood pressure.   (D)

9 Signs and symptoms of an asthma attack include

    I shortness of breath.

    II coughing.

    III wheezing.

    IV vomiting.

(A) I and II only   (A)

(B) II and III only   (B)

(C) I, II and III only   (C)

(D) II, III and IV only   (D)

10 Which of the following is NOT an effect of asthma on the respiratory tract?

(A) increased mucus secretion   (A)

(B) inflammation of the bronchial lining   (B)

(C) narrowing of the bronchi and bronchioles   (C)

(D) rupturing of the walls of the alveoli   (D)

11 An obese person is also likely to suffer from

    I hypertension.

    II type I diabetes mellitus.

    III type II diabetes mellitus.

    IV coronary heart disease.

(A) I and IV only   (A)

(B) II and III only   (B)

(C) I, II and IV only   (C)

(D) I, III and IV only   (D)

12 Type I diabetes mellitus occurs when

(A) the pancreas does not produce insulin. Ⓐ

(B) cells in the body do not respond to insulin. Ⓑ

(C) a person becomes overweight. Ⓒ

(D) a person becomes old. Ⓓ

13 Which of the following is NOT a long-term benefit of exercise on the body?

(A) increase in muscle size Ⓐ

(B) a lower resting heart rate Ⓑ

(C) more efficient gaseous exchange Ⓒ

(D) a slower metabolic rate Ⓓ

14 Pneumonia is most commonly caused by a

(A) virus. Ⓐ

(B) fungus. Ⓑ

(C) bacterium. Ⓒ

(D) protozoan. Ⓓ

15 Which of the following diseases can be transmitted to others when an infected person sneezes in a crowded place?

    I cholera

    II typhoid

    III influenza

    IV tuberculosis

(A) I and II only Ⓐ

(B) III and IV only Ⓑ

(C) I, II and III only Ⓒ

(D) II, III and IV only Ⓓ

16 Fungicide ointments would be BEST used to treat

(A) herpes.   (A)

(B) typhoid.   (B)

(C) ringworm.   (C)

(D) gastroenteritis.   (D)

17 Which option in the table below shows the CORRECT indicators of gonorrhoea, syphilis and genital herpes?

	Gonorrhoea	Syphilis	Genital herpes	
(A)	pus discharge in urine	skin rash and sores	genital blisters and ulcers	(A)
(B)	blood discharge in urine	blindness	pus discharge in urine	(B)
(C)	blood discharge in urine	skin rash and sores	pus discharge in urine	(C)
(D)	pus discharge in urine	blindness	genital blisters and ulcers	(D)

18 Which of the following are ways in which HIV/AIDS is transmitted?

    I by receiving blood from an infected person

    II by sharing eating utensils with an infected person

    III from an infected mother to her baby during breastfeeding

    IV by having unprotected sexual intercourse with an infected person

(A) I and II only   (A)

(B) II and IV only   (B)

(C) I, III and IV only   (C)

(D) I, II, III and IV   (D)

19 Which statement below about HIV/AIDS is TRUE?

    (A) Vaccination is an effective prevention strategy.   Ⓐ

    (B) It can be treated using anti-retroviral drugs.   Ⓑ

    (C) The Caribbean has a relatively low infection rate.   Ⓒ

    (D) All individuals experience signs and symptoms within a few weeks of infection.   Ⓓ

20 The spread of HIV/AIDS can be controlled by

    (A) vaccination.   Ⓐ

    (B) condom use.   Ⓑ

    (C) penicillin injections.   Ⓒ

    (D) adding chlorine to drinking water.   Ⓓ

21 Stillbirths are MOST likely to result from a mother being infected with

    (A) HIV/AIDS.   Ⓐ

    (B) syphilis.   Ⓑ

    (C) gonorrhoea.   Ⓒ

    (D) genital herpes.   Ⓓ

22 Which of the following is NOT a socio-economic impact of diseases on the Caribbean population?

    (A) increased demand on health services   Ⓐ

    (B) reduced foreign exchange earnings   Ⓑ

    (C) reduced productivity of businesses   Ⓒ

    (D) improved standard of living   Ⓓ

Items 23–24 refer to the table below which shows some of the major causes of death in the Caribbean in 1985 and 2000.

Cause of death	% deaths in 1985	% deaths in 2000
heart disease	17	16
stroke	13	10
cancers	13	15
diabetes	6	10
hypertension	5	6
HIV/AIDS	no data available	6

23 Which causes of death have decreased during the period shown?

(A) heart disease and cancers   Ⓐ

(B) diabetes and stroke   Ⓑ

(C) heart disease and stroke   Ⓒ

(D) diabetes and hypertension   Ⓓ

24 What is the MOST likely reason there was no data available for HIV/AIDS in 1985?

(A) The virus that causes AIDS did not exist in 1985.   Ⓐ

(B) Too many people had already died from HIV/AIDS.   Ⓑ

(C) HIV/AIDS was not contributing to deaths in 1985.   Ⓒ

(D) The virus that causes AIDS was only discovered a few years before 1985.   Ⓓ

1 Which option in the table below CORRECTLY shows the causative agents of malaria and dengue fever?

	Malaria	Dengue fever
(A)	protozoan	bacterium
(B)	fungus	virus
(C)	protozoan	virus
(D)	bacterium	protozoan

(A)
(B)
(C)
(D)

2 The *Anopheles* mosquito is known to transmit

(A) malaria.

(B) yellow fever.

(C) dengue fever.

(D) gastroenteritis.

Ⓐ
Ⓑ
Ⓒ
Ⓓ

3 Which of the following are signs and symptoms of dengue fever?

   I rash

   II jaundice

   III kidney failure

   IV muscle and joint pains

(A) I and II only

(B) I and IV only

(C) II and III only

(D) I, II and IV only

Ⓐ
Ⓑ
Ⓒ
Ⓓ

4 An organism that carries a disease agent and transmits the disease agent from one host to another is a

(A) pathogen. (A)

(B) parasite. (B)

(C) vector. (C)

(D) virus. (D)

Item 5 refers to the diagram below, which shows a map of a town with four main housing developments, labelled A–D.

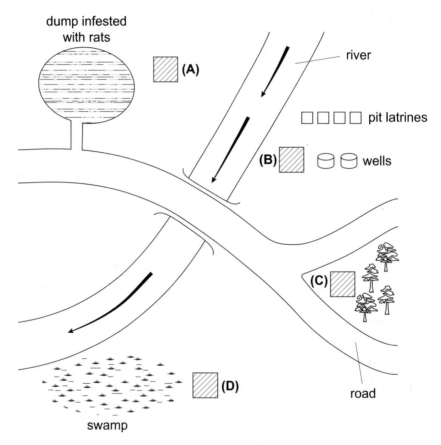

5 In which housing development are the residents MOST likely to suffer from leptospirosis?

(A) (A)

(B) (B)

(C) (C)

(D) (D)

6 Which of the following are ways by which houseflies transmit diseases?

      I by biting a person and injecting saliva

      II by defecating on food

      III while walking on food

      IV while feeding

(**A**) I and II only   Ⓐ

(**B**) II and III only   Ⓑ

(**C**) I, II and IV only   Ⓒ

(**D**) II, III and IV only   Ⓓ

Item 7 refers to the stages in the life cycle of a housefly shown below.

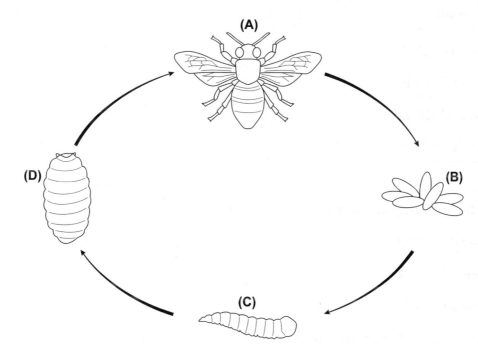

7 Which stage causes bacterial contamination of food?

(**A**)   Ⓐ

(**B**)   Ⓑ

(**C**)   Ⓒ

(**D**)   Ⓓ

8 The correct sequence of the stages in the life cycle of a mosquito is

(A) pupa $\longrightarrow$ adult $\longrightarrow$ egg $\longrightarrow$ larva   Ⓐ

(B) adult $\longrightarrow$ egg $\longrightarrow$ larva $\longrightarrow$ pupa   Ⓑ

(C) larva $\longrightarrow$ egg $\longrightarrow$ pupa $\longrightarrow$ adult   Ⓒ

(D) egg $\longrightarrow$ pupa $\longrightarrow$ larva $\longrightarrow$ adult   Ⓓ

9 Which stages of the life cycle of a mosquito are directly affected by the draining of stagnant water?

    I pupa

    II egg

    III larva

    IV adult

(A) I and II only   Ⓐ

(B) II and III only   Ⓑ

(C) I, II and III only   Ⓒ

(D) I, III and IV only   Ⓓ

10 All of the following are methods used to control the spread of leptospirosis, EXCEPT

(A) rodent control.   Ⓐ

(B) public education.   Ⓑ

(C) spraying with insecticides.   Ⓒ

(D) vaccination of domestic animals.   Ⓓ

11 Maintaining personal hygiene is important in order to

      I prevent infections.

      II eliminate body odours.

     III ensure good health.

     IV promote social acceptance.

(A) I and II only   Ⓐ

(B) II and III only   Ⓑ

(C) I, II and III only   Ⓒ

(D) I, II, III and IV   Ⓓ

12 Which of the following is NOT a measure used to maintain personal hygiene?

(A) male circumcision   Ⓐ

(B) using a deodorant   Ⓑ

(C) washing hands once per day   Ⓒ

(D) brushing teeth twice per day   Ⓓ

13 Sterilisation is defined as

(A) the cleaning of a surface using chemicals.   Ⓐ

(B) isolation of a single strain of a microorganism.   Ⓑ

(C) the removal of some of the microorganisms present.   Ⓒ

(D) the complete destruction of all the microorganisms present.   Ⓓ

14 Which of the following are methods of sterilisation?

      I boiling

     II pasteurisation

    III autoclaving

    IV deep freezing

  (A) I and II only   Ⓐ

  (B) II and III only   Ⓑ

  (C) I, II and III only   Ⓒ

  (D) I, II and IV only   Ⓓ

15 High temperatures protect food from microorganisms by

  (A) lowering the pH until microorganisms cannot function.   Ⓐ

  (B) killing microorganisms and their spores.   Ⓑ

  (C) removing oxygen needed for aerobic respiration.   Ⓒ

  (D) slowing the growth of microorganisms.   Ⓓ

16 Which statement about disinfectants and antiseptics is CORRECT?

  (A) They are used in the same way.   Ⓐ

  (B) Disinfectants are used to kill pathogens on living tissue and antiseptics are used to kill pathogens on non-living surfaces.   Ⓑ

  (C) Disinfectants are used to kill pathogens on non-living surfaces and antiseptics are used to kill pathogens on living tissue.   Ⓒ

  (D) Disinfectants kill some pathogens and antiseptics kill all pathogens on contact.   Ⓓ

17 Which of the following would be used to treat a bacterial infection?

(A) antiseptics   Ⓐ

(B) antibiotics   Ⓑ

(C) antiviral agents   Ⓒ

(D) antifungal agents   Ⓓ

Item 18 refers to the following diagram of a disease-causing microorganism and a defence mechanism produced by the body.

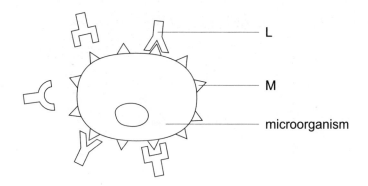

18 Which option in the table correctly identifies L and M?

	L	M
(A)	antibody	antigen
(B)	antigen	antibody
(C)	anti-toxin	antibody
(D)	antibody	anti-toxin

Ⓐ
Ⓑ
Ⓒ
Ⓓ

Items 19–20 refer to the following options.

   (A) natural active immunity

   (B) natural passive immunity

   (C) artificial active immunity

   (D) artificial passive immunity

Match EACH item below with one of the options above. Each option may be used once, more than once or not at all.

19 The type of immunity provided by breastfeeding.

   (A)   Ⓐ

   (B)   Ⓑ

   (C)   Ⓒ

   (D)   Ⓓ

20 The type of immunity gained when a person is given a serum containing antibodies.

   (A)   Ⓐ

   (B)   Ⓑ

   (C)   Ⓒ

   (D)   Ⓓ

21 Which statement below is INCORRECT?

   (A) Vaccination provides acquired immunity.   Ⓐ

   (B) Immunity is the body's resistance to disease.   Ⓑ

   (C) A vaccine contains antigens that stimulate active immunity.   Ⓒ

   (D) Immunity is the same as immunisation.   Ⓓ

22 Active immunity to a disease is produced

    (A) by taking antibiotics.   (A)

    (B) by being injected with antibodies.   (B)

    (C) when a foetus gets antibodies across the placenta.   (C)

    (D) by becoming infected with a disease and recovering from it.   (D)

23 When a person takes a drug over a period of time and needs the drug in order to function, this is called

    (A) dependence.   (A)

    (B) withdrawal.   (B)

    (C) tolerance.   (C)

    (D) desire.   (D)

24 Drugs that are prescribed by a doctor to help someone sleep are called

    (A) stimulants.   (A)

    (B) sedatives.   (B)

    (C) painkillers.   (C)

    (D) hallucinogens.   (D)

25 A drug that causes users to see images, hear sounds and experience sensations that are not real is a

    (A) stimulant.   (A)

    (B) depressant.   (B)

    (C) hallucinogen.   (C)

    (D) narcotic.   (D)

26 Short-term effects of alcohol abuse on the body include

      I slurred speech.

      II faster reflexes.

     III dehydration.

     IV cirrhosis of the liver.

(A) I and III only   Ⓐ

(B) II and IV only   Ⓑ

(C) I, III and IV only   Ⓒ

(D) I, II, III and IV   Ⓓ

27 Which of the following is/are social effect(s) of drug misuse?

      I Increased demand on health services.

     II Increased crime rate.

    III Lower suicide rate.

(A) II only   Ⓐ

(B) I and II only   Ⓑ

(C) II and III only   Ⓒ

(D) I, II and III   Ⓓ

Item 28 refers to the table below, which shows the results of a study that examined the effects of drug misuse in the workplace.

Effect of drug misuse	% of respondents
impaired performance	55
frequent absences	50
disciplinary problems	48
intoxication at work	45
job loss	40

28 If there were 300 respondents in the study group, how many respondents had impaired performance due to drug use?

(A) 200   Ⓐ

(B) 165   Ⓑ

(C) 150   Ⓒ

(D) 55   Ⓓ

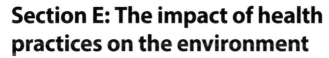

Section E: The impact of health practices on the environment
E1: Pollution and water

1 A pollutant is BEST defined as

(A) an organism that causes disease.   Ⓐ

(B) a poisonous type of domestic waste.   Ⓑ

(C) an unwanted substance that is disposed of in the environment.   Ⓒ

(D) a harmful substance or form of energy that is released into the environment.   Ⓓ

2 The following are air pollutants, EXCEPT

(A) nitrates.   Ⓐ

(B) volatile organic compounds.   Ⓑ

(C) sulfur dioxide.   Ⓒ

(D) carbon monoxide.   Ⓓ

3 Air pollution from industry contributes to

      I acid rain.

      II eutrophication.

      III global warming.

(A) I and II only   Ⓐ

(B) I and III only   Ⓑ

(C) II and III only   Ⓒ

(D) I, II and III   Ⓓ

4 Which of the activities listed below contribute directly to water pollution?

      I Use of chemical fertilisers.

      II Use of agricultural pesticides.

      III Dumping of refuse in waterways.

      IV Burning of fossil fuels in motor vehicles.

(A) I and III only   Ⓐ

(B) I and IV only   Ⓑ

(C) I, II and III only   Ⓒ

(D) II, III and IV only   Ⓓ

5 Which of the following is NOT an effect of air pollution on human beings?

(A) typhoid   Ⓐ

(B) lung cancer   Ⓑ

(C) eye irritation   Ⓒ

(D) asthma attack   Ⓓ

6 The addition of excess nutrients to water that stimulate algal growth is called

(A) sedimentation. (A)

(B) eutrophication. (B)

(C) coral bleaching. (C)

(D) bioaccumulation. (D)

7 Water pollution may be controlled by

    I using non-biodegradable detergents.

    II proper sewage treatment.

    III stricter laws and penalties.

    IV public education.

(A) I and II only (A)

(B) III and IV only (B)

(C) I, II and III only (C)

(D) II, III and IV only (D)

8 Which of the following methods can be used to reduce global warming?

    I Planting more trees.

    II Building more factories.

    III Using alternative energy sources.

(A) I and II only (A)

(B) I and III only (B)

(C) II and III only (C)

(D) I, II and III (D)

Items **9–10** refer to the water cycle shown below.

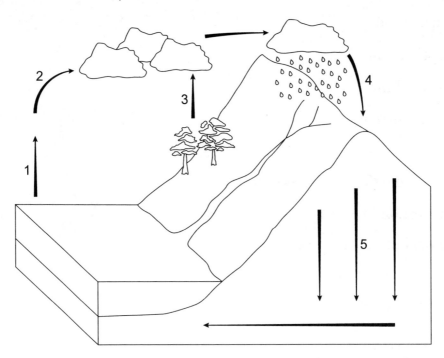

9 The process labelled 3 is

(A) condensation. Ⓐ

(B) precipitation. Ⓑ

(C) transpiration. Ⓒ

(D) infiltration. Ⓓ

10 The energy needed for the process labelled 1 to take place is provided by

(A) the wind. Ⓐ

(B) the Sun. Ⓑ

(C) the river. Ⓒ

(D) heat from the Earth. Ⓓ

11 Which of the following methods may be suggested by a Public Health Nurse for water treatment at home?

> **I** boiling
>
> **II** filtering
>
> **III** freezing
>
> **IV** adding chlorine sterilizing tablets

(A) I and II only   Ⓐ

(B) II and IV only   Ⓑ

(C) I, II and III only   Ⓒ

(D) I, II and IV only   Ⓓ

12 Which of the following is NOT a step used when testing water for bacteria?

(A) Collect a water sample in a sterile container.   Ⓐ

(B) Pour a small amount of water onto an agar plate.   Ⓑ

(C) Refrigerate the agar plate for 24 hours.   Ⓒ

(D) Incubate the agar plate at 35 °C for 24 hours.   Ⓓ

13 How many colonies of coliform bacteria will be found in water that is considered safe for drinking?

(A) 0   Ⓐ

(B) 1–5   Ⓑ

(C) 6–10   Ⓒ

(D) 11–15   Ⓓ

Item 14 refers to the processes involved in the large-scale purification of drinking water listed below.

    1 filtration

    2 chlorination

    3 sedimentation

    4 screening

14 Which option below shows the correct order in which these processes are carried out?

    (A) 1, 2, 3, 4   Ⓐ

    (B) 3, 4, 1, 2   Ⓑ

    (C) 4, 3, 1, 2   Ⓒ

    (D) 4, 1, 2, 3   Ⓓ

15 Which process in water purification involves the removal of large suspended solids?

    (A) filtration   Ⓐ

    (B) screening   Ⓑ

    (C) chlorination   Ⓒ

    (D) sedimentation   Ⓓ

16 Human activities affect water supplies by causing

    I loss of potable water.

    II reduction of freshwater supplies.

    III higher cost of water treatment.

    (A) I only   Ⓐ

    (B) I and II only   Ⓑ

    (C) II and III only   Ⓒ

    (D) I, II and III   Ⓓ

17 Which of the following is/are associated with contaminated water?

    I bronchitis

    II diarrhoea

    III mercury poisoning

(A) II only   Ⓐ

(B) I and III only   Ⓑ

(C) II and III only   Ⓒ

(D) I, II and III   Ⓓ

18 Lead poisoning may result in

(A) brain damage.   Ⓐ

(B) emphysema.   Ⓑ

(C) lung cancer.   Ⓒ

(D) obesity.   Ⓓ

E2: Sewage and solid waste disposal

1 Which of the following substances is/are usually found in sewage?

    I rainwater

    II human faeces

    III laundry waste

(A) II only   Ⓐ

(B) I and II only   Ⓑ

(C) II and III only   Ⓒ

(D) I, II and III   Ⓓ

2 Which of the following options CORRECTLY identifies proper and improper sewage disposal practices?

	Proper sewage disposal practice	Improper sewage disposal practice	
(A)	sewage is released onto the land	sewage is released into treatment ponds	Ⓐ
(B)	sewage is released into treatment ponds	sewage is released into open water	Ⓑ
(C)	sewage is removed from buildings through pipes	sewage is released into treatment ponds	Ⓒ
(D)	sewage is released into open water	sewage is released onto the land	Ⓓ

3 Improper sewage disposal may result in

    I eutrophication of rivers.

    II contamination of drinking water.

    III spread of water-borne diseases.

    IV disruption of aquatic food chains.

(A) I and II only   Ⓐ

(B) III and IV only   Ⓑ

(C) I, II and III only   Ⓒ

(D) I, II, III and IV   Ⓓ

4 Which of the following are stages in the activated sludge method of sewage treatment?

    I Processing of sludge to make methane or fertiliser.

    II Mixing compressed air with aerobic bacteria in aeration tanks.

    III Screening to remove large objects.

    IV Spraying sewage onto stones covered with aerobic bacteria and protozoa.

(A) I and II only   Ⓐ

(B) I, II and III only   Ⓑ

(C) I, III and IV only   Ⓒ

(D) II, III and IV only   Ⓓ

5 The activated sludge and biological filter methods of sewage treatment both involve

    (A) the use of aerobic microorganisms to break down organic matter.   (A)

    (B) spraying sewage over stones covered with bacteria.   (B)

    (C) mixing compressed air with the sewage.   (C)

    (D) the use of disinfectants to kill bacteria.   (D)

Items 6–7 refer to the diagram below of a pit latrine.

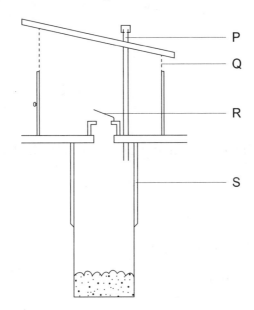

6 Which structure allows gases produced in the pit to escape?

    (A) P   (A)

    (B) Q   (B)

    (C) R   (C)

    (D) S   (D)

7 What is the function of the structure labelled R?

    (A) It is a seat.   (A)

    (B) To keep out flies and rats.   (B)

    (C) To allow circulation of air.   (C)

    (D) To allow liquids to drain from the pit.   (D)

8 Which of the following statements about siting and constructing a pit latrine is/are CORRECT?

      I Sandy soil is most suitable.

     II The pit should be at least 1 metre deep.

    III The latrine should be close to a reservoir.

    IV The latrine should be positioned downhill from water sources.

(A) II only   Ⓐ

(B) I and III only   Ⓑ

(C) I and IV only   Ⓒ

(D) I, III and IV only   Ⓓ

9 All of the following are benefits of using pit latrines in the Caribbean, EXCEPT

(A) they do not contribute to groundwater pollution.   Ⓐ

(B) they can be used as a source of biomass.   Ⓑ

(C) they require less water than flush toilets.   Ⓒ

(D) they are relatively cheap to construct.   Ⓓ

10 Domestic refuse is BEST defined as

(A) wastewater from homes.   Ⓐ

(B) all the organic matter produced in the home.   Ⓑ

(C) all unwanted metals discarded from the home.   Ⓒ

(D) all unwanted solids that accumulate after use in the home.   Ⓓ

11 Advantages of incineration include

    I contribution to global warming.

    II reduction in the volume of refuse.

    III waste heat can be used to heat water.

(A) I and II only   Ⓐ

(B) I and III only   Ⓑ

(C) II and III only   Ⓒ

(D) I, II and III   Ⓓ

12 The BEST method to dispose of plant material in household waste is

(A) reusing.   Ⓐ

(B) composting.   Ⓑ

(C) incineration.   Ⓒ

(D) dumping in a landfill.   Ⓓ

13 The function of the bottom liner of a landfill is to

(A) prevent liquids from the waste seeping into soil and water.   Ⓐ

(B) prevent the escape of gases into the atmosphere.   Ⓑ

(C) prevent the entry of vectors.   Ⓒ

(D) trap the solid waste.   Ⓓ

14 Which of the following is/are reason(s) for compaction of refuse at a landfill?

    I To reduce the volume of the refuse.

    II To make it difficult for vectors to penetrate.

    III To reduce the amount of bacteria in the landfill.

(A) I only   Ⓐ

(B) II only   Ⓑ

(C) I and II only   Ⓒ

(D) II and III only   Ⓓ

15 Which method below is the MOST environmentally friendly way to dispose of solid waste in the Caribbean?

(A) recycling   Ⓐ

(B) incineration   Ⓑ

(C) using landfills   Ⓒ

(D) dumping into the ocean   Ⓓ

16 Improper disposal of solid waste contributes to all of the following, EXCEPT

(A) offensive odours.   Ⓐ

(B) obstruction of drains.   Ⓑ

(C) increase in biodiversity.   Ⓒ

(D) pollution of air, land and water.   Ⓓ

Items 17–18 refer to the graph below, which shows diseases/conditions suffered by residents living nearby and far away from an open dump site.

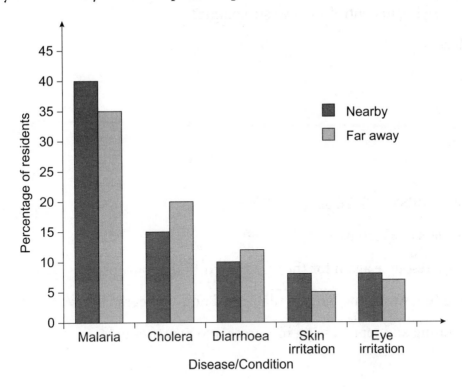

17 Based on the information presented, the greatest impact of having an open dump in a nearby community is

(A) it is extremely noisy. (A)

(B) it releases air pollutants. (B)

(C) it releases water pollutants. (C)

(D) it is a breeding place for vectors of disease. (D)

18 Which diseases/conditions are residents who live far from the dump MORE likely to suffer from when compared to those who live near to the dump?

(A) malaria and cholera (A)

(B) cholera and diarrhoea (B)

(C) diarrhoea and eye irritation (C)

(D) skin irritation and eye irritation (D)

19 Miss Joyce carries a cloth shopping bag when she goes to the supermarket, instead of taking the plastic bags they offer. Which of the following BEST describes the method she is employing to control solid waste volume?

(A) reduce   Ⓐ

(B) reuse   Ⓑ

(C) recycle   Ⓒ

(D) repair   Ⓓ

20 Recycling is BEST defined as

(A) using less of a resource.   Ⓐ

(B) using a resource again for the same or a different purpose.   Ⓑ

(C) separating waste into biodegradable and non-biodegradable materials.   Ⓒ

(D) separating and reprocessing resources into new products.   Ⓓ

21 Biodegradable substances

(A) can be broken down by sunlight into harmless materials.   Ⓐ

(B) can be broken down by microorganisms into harmless materials.   Ⓑ

(C) can be broken down by chemicals into harmless materials.   Ⓒ

(D) cannot be broken down by any means into harmless materials.   Ⓓ

22 Which of the following items is biodegradable?

(A) a rubber tyre   Ⓐ

(B) a glass bottle   Ⓑ

(C) a wooden stool   Ⓒ

(D) an aluminium can   Ⓓ